Mystique and Identity

Mystique and Identity:
Women's Fashions of the 1950s

Barbara A. Schreier

The Chrysler Museum
Norfolk, Virginia
February 2 - March 18, 1984

Cover:

Jewelry, Courtesy of Hardy's, Inc.:
  Platinum diamond emerald ring —
    a 2.28 carat emerald and 28 full cut
    diamonds.
  Platinum diamond bracelet —
    186 full cut diamonds, 18 brilliant cut
    diamonds and 9 baguette cut diamonds.

Model: Botetourt Spot

Photograph: Brooks Johnson

© 1984 The Chrysler Museum
Library of Congress Number 83-63525
ISBN 0-940744-45-7
Catalogue Design: Germaine Clair

Acknowledgements

I would like to acknowledge the great debt that I owe to The Chrysler Museum. Special thanks are extended to the Director, David W. Steadman, for his conviction that clothes are more than decorative objects. To Thomas W. Sokolowski, Chief Curator and guiding spirit, I offer my heartfelt appreciation. His unerring good taste and marvelous tongue-in-chic [sic] wit made this project a joy. I thank Amy Ciccone for all her support, and Troy Moss and Catherine Jordan for their professionalism and graciousness. To Mark Clark, who patiently responded to all requests and shared my love of historic clothing, thank you. I have only the highest praise for the staff of The Chrysler Museum. The quality of the catalogue photographs attests to the excellent work of Brooks Johnson and Jennifer Hobgood, and the high standards of the Art Preparators and Dan Mitchell and the maintenance staff are greatly appreciated. I also acknowledge the great debt that I owe to Linda Austin. Her help was crucial to every phase of the exhibit; this long distance project would have been impossible without her skilled assistance. To all of the librarians who were so patient and helpful with my many requests, thank you. I am particularly grateful to the librarians at the Fashion Institute of Technology, the Costume Institute, and Smith College. The staff at the J. Walter Thompson Company deserves special recognition for their generous assistance with this project. My thanks also go to all of the individuals who loaned the accessories which provided the essential finishing touches; to Mr. and Mrs. Schantz of People's Cleaners, for their meticulous handling and cleaning of the costumes; the Freemason-Blue Bonnet Hatworks and Miller & Rhoads Department Store for their generous loan of mannequins for the photography sessions; to Betty Bippus Graham, Fashion Director of Leggett Department Store; Pat Hoke of Miller & Rhoads; John Parker of The Kirn Memorial Library; Chanel, Inc.; and Terry Albert. I am deeply indebted to Martha Caldwell, who will always be my most important mentor, and to Honore David, for her invaluable introductions. This catalogue is dedicated to my husband, Donald E. Drake II. It is his steadfast love which supports and fosters my own search for identity.

Barbara A. Schreier

We were emerging from a period of war, of uniforms, of women-soldiers built like boxers. I drew women-flowers, soft shoulders, flowering busts, fine waists like liana and wide skirts like corolla.

Christian Dior[1]

The years following the end of World War II witnessed an important shift in the definition of feminine beauty. The history of dress is synonymous with the study of the cyclical permutations of style, so change itself is hardly remarkable. Yet, post-war fashions deviated from the normal evolutionary pattern by its revolutionary nature. The stirrings of change had begun in the late 1930s, but this movement was halted by the war and remained dormant until Christian Dior's first collection in 1947, when it exploded in full form.

The New Look featured rounded bosoms and hips, gently curving shoulders, sweeping hemlines, and tiny waists, reducing the female silhouette to a series of undulating curves. It was extravagantly romantic — the perfect answer for millions of women seeking release from the mannish angularity of wartime fashions. This was the triumphant beginning of the fashions of the 1950s — a decade that saw the celebration of femininity evolve into a cult. It was an age of elaborate accessories, precise make-up, and choreographed mannerisms which glorified the sophisticated lady. Throughout the 1950s, fashion helped to balance woman on her pedestal by reinforcing her dependent role and surrounding her in an elegant aura.

The precariousness of this position is evident when one follows the tides of fashions through the 1960s. Within a handful of years, the trend shifted and the ideal fashionable form was once again redefined. During the sixties, fashion devoted itself to youth, leaving the mature woman behind to lament the passing of her prime. The unstructured styles of designers such as Courrèges, Mary Quant, and Pierre Cardin depended more for their success upon a firm, youthful body and less on the garment's decorative qualities. The privileged elite lost their sanctioning power as the traditional fashion pyramid toppled and the mood shifted from serious formality to a playful, and often eccentric, informality. In their struggle to emulate the androgynous shape popularized by Twiggy, women discarded the padded curves

which dominated fashions in the fifties. Sandwiched in between the masculine silhouette of the early forties and the boyish shape of the sixties, fashions of the fifties stand out as a revival of feminine opulence.

Any attempt to explore the deeper meanings embodied in women's dress of the late 1940s and 1950s must consider the effect of the post-war years on women's lives and the emergence of the "feminine mystique."[2] In an effort to regain a sense of normalcy, men and women worked to restore pre-war sex roles. Central to this movement was a commitment to preserve the home and family as effective buffers against the confusion of the changing world. Woman's responsibilities as mother, wife, and guardian of moral stability were clearly spelled out. A well-defined identity held considerable appeal for the many individuals who were struggling with the bewilderment of post-war adjustment.

Reinstitution of these traditional values demanded a renunciation of the assertive role women had assumed during the war, because it was perceived as undermining domestic happiness. In 1950 Agnes Meyer wrote, "What modern woman has to recapture is the wisdom that just being a woman is her central task and her greatest honor."[3] Vogue published an article in 1946 that carried specific instructions for women intent on climbing back up on the pedestal. Readers were urged to "stop making decisions ... stop driving the car like Eisenhower's WAC, develop a sudden inability to balance our checkbook" and to "memorize once more the age-old

formula for a woman: a utensil whose potentialities for good hard wear are artfully disguised in a smoke screen of frivolity."[4]

The ideology of this feminine mystique stood in direct contrast to the realities of women's wartime roles. During World War II, millions of women moved out of the home and into the workforce out of necessity and patriotic duty. Yet at the close of the war, the nation took a second look at the issue of female employment. The question was whether or not women should actively pursue a career and independence outside of the home. Experts answered with a resounding "No," arguing that the only fulfilling career for a woman was the role of housewife and mother. Women who assumed any other role were accused of exhibiting aberrant behavior ranging from unfemininity to subversiveness. The issue was attacked from all sides, constantly confronting a woman with an unrelenting assessment of her character based solely on her sex. The individual woman was rarely discussed. Instead, the outpouring of voices grouped all of the problems as one — women's dilemma.

Ferdinand Lundberg and Marynia Farnham presented one of the strongest cases for a woman's rightful place in the home in their book Modern Woman: The Lost Sex.[5] According to the authors, the more women turned away from femininity, the more discontented they became. Only by following her "natural" vocation could a woman hope to achieve the highest level of happiness and satisfaction. Higher education and careers

figure 1.
Adrian Suit
Courtesy *Vogue* © 1943 (renewed 1971), by The Condé Nast Publications, Inc.

figure 2.
Dior's "New Look"
Courtesy *Vogue* © 1947 (renewed 1975), by The Condé Nast Publications, Inc.

were viewed with scepticism as potential enemies of the family, since they often led to the masculinization of women. The consequences spelled disaster not only for the individual and her family, but for the entire society.

The mystique was more than the rhetoric of a group of "experts." It became the new social ethic of the fifties, with the domestication of the American female as its central theme. The stay-at-home ideology received strong support from popular women's magazines and books in their glorification of the passive housewife. Advertisers reinforced the doctrine that woman's highest function in life was to care for her husband and children. The formula worked largely because it carried substantial appeal at a time when traditional ideas were gaining new influence.[6]

Yet, the mystique was suffocating to women who found the carefully defined pattern too restrictive and the walls of their homes too confining. In her analysis of the situation, Betty Friedan charged that women were victimized by the self-perpetuating myth of American culture that defined feminine happiness only in terms of a total involvement with the home. The image of the passive woman left no room for other options, so individuals with a wish for something more were without support. The decade took on a frantic desperation as men and women tried to live up to a dream that could not succeed. In *The Feminine Mystique*, Friedan documented the growing dissatisfaction of women who found the mystique smothering and whose unhappiness was exacerbated by

their feelings of guilt and failure.[7] The problems festered throughout the fifties with increasing numbers of casualties, yet the home remained the central focus for the vast majority of middle-class women.

The ideal woman of the fifties was not to be the sole daytime occupant of that home. The chidren's rhyme "First comes love, then comes marriage, then comes baby in the baby carriage" became the mantra of post-war society. Following on the heels of a marriage boom came the army of the baby explosion. Americans, bolstered by a renewed faith in the future and sustained by a healthy economy, joined together in a nationwide affirmation of what Landon Jones described as the "Procreation Ethic."[8] Couples, accepting the cultural norm that made childlessness deviant behavior, worked at becoming parents. Beginning with a post-war surge of babies in 1946, the baby boom continued through 1964, reaching its peak in 1957. During that nineteen year period, 76,441,000 babies were born, or one-third of the population in 1980.[9] This period is also marked by an increase in the size of the American family. Between the years 1940 and 1960, the birthrate for third children doubled and that for fourth children tripled.

The formidable responsibilities of parenthood largely rested with the mother demanding her constant attention. Women were expected to adjust to a burgeoning family with an appropriate expansion of energy and sense of achievement, yet for many it became harder and harder to keep up. In this

child-oriented society, expectations of maternal nurturing became a national crusade. Responding to these pressures, most women rose to accept the Spockian challenge: "You have the capacity to rear a genius, a masterpiece. Such an activity should therefore rightfully absorb all of your time and energy."[10]

During the fifties, raising children necessitated not only the proper attitude, but the proper environment as well. Paralleling the increasing importance of the family unit during this period was Americans' migration to suburbia. The boundaries of these rigidly planned communities provided the setting for hundreds of thousands of white, middle-class families.[11] Although the suburban concept existed well before World War II, it was not until the fifties that the movement became a widespread middle-class phenomenon. The federal government supported and encouraged the trend by guaranteeing mortgages featuring low down payments and long amortization plans.[12] The planned communities attracted couples with similar backgrounds, interests, and goals. Recognizing that prospective buyers were interested in purchasing a lifestyle and sense of belonging as well as a residence, developers highlighted these advantages in their promotional advertising:

> A cup of coffee — symbol of PARK FOREST! Coffee pots bubble all day long in Park Forest. This sign of friendliness tells you how much neighbors enjoy each other's company — feel glad that they can share their daily joys — yes, and troubles, too.[13]

Mass-produced single family housing plans featuring limited options in floorplans, size, color, and design encouraged a conformist spirit by creating a homogeneous exterior setting. Open interiors with fewer doors and big picture windows discouraged family privacy.

The suburban lifestyle also introduced a new dimension into woman's role by modifying the structure of the housewife's day. She now was expected to assume the additional responsibilities of community involvement. Thanks to the labor-saving devices surrounding the suburban woman, she could fill her days with volunteer work and PTA meetings and still have time to preserve the sanctity of her home as a nurturing oasis. These activities were a part of the suburban socialization process designed to complement, but compete with, the

figure 3.
Air Raid Warden
Courtesy *Vogue* © 1942 (renewed 1970), by The Condé Nast Publications, Inc.

figure 4.
This is one of those days I feel I really accomplished something.
Cartoon by Mary Gibson.

smooth functioning of the home. Even weekend activities were centered around the benefits and demands of home ownership, mingling backyard barbecues with gardening, lawn maintenance, and do-it-yourself projects.[14] Adjustment to the norm was essential to this spirit of group participation, so deviation was actively discouraged.

The fifties' vision of woman's place in the home bears a striking resemblance to the expectations surrounding the Victorian woman. In both instances, women were elevated to the role of protector of the moral, spiritual, and physical well-being of her family.[15] Conversely, women were admonished to avoid excessive involvement with the outside world, since it was perceived to be the male's domain. This essay written in 1950 could just have easily been written 100 years earlier when the world was struggling to make sense out of the industrial revolution:

> Surface influences of a competitive, materialistic world have observed the importance of women's role as the repository of continuity and of purposeful living derived from their biological and social functions. Our technological civilization has atrophied their emotions, and nothing is more horrible than a woman whose instinctive reactions have been destroyed.[16]

There is, however, a critical difference which separates the post-war pedestal from its Victorian predecessor. In the nineteenth century, the enshrined lady was a member of the leisured class with an army of servants who provided the free time required to pursue the ideal.

However, the homemaker of the 1950s was not only the executive of her household, she was the staff as well. Even the woman who could afford outside help opted to take care of the house herself.

One of the tenets of the mystique was that housework was not drudgery, but rather the ultimate source of creative expression. The American housewife was flattered, cajoled, and pressured into acknowledging the special sense of achievement that comes from a sparkling home, clean laundry, and a healthy family. For those tasks which fell short of creative standards, there was an endless assortment of specialized products to ease the monotony and relieve the housewife's burden.[17] In this economy of abundances, dishwashers, dryers and electric mixers were readily available to help women redefine the home as the artist's studio.[18]

The timing was ripe for this new age of consumerism. By 1948, economic recovery was well under way and people were beginning to talk of a prosperity that had no end in sight. It seemed to millions of Americans that the good life had finally arrived. The public's demand for visible signs of progress kept expanding, and manufacturers accelerated production rates to meet these needs. In keeping with the spirit of the new age, the mere activity of buying came to represent happiness. Purchasing on credit and installment plans were the acceptable way to procure the trappings of success in this consumption-oriented society where the price tag of one's home, car and clothing was the measure of a person's worth.

One of the most visible signs of progress and a dominant feature of the home during the 1950s was the television set. The prevailing domestic scenario of the 1940s in which families clustered around the radio quickly became outmoded. The new focal point was the television set where friends and families gathered to catch the latest episode of such favorite programs as "I Love Lucy," "The Ed Sullivan Show," "Mr. Peepers," and "Your Show of Shows."[19] A wide spectrum of programming promised something for every member of the family. Dramas, documentaries, situation comedies, variety shows, game shows, and musical varieties were all available at a reasonable price without ever leaving home. Americans developed an insatiable appetite for this entertainment form, until, by 1956, they spent as much time watching television as they did on their jobs.[20] Frozen TV dinners were introduced to ensure that food preparation and consumption would not interrupt an evening's viewing. The reality of accessible entertainment, the visible reinforcement of middle-class values, and the immediacy of the message all worked together to make television an enticing commodity. The trend increased as the decade advanced so that by 1960, in the United States alone, there were fifty million television sets in operation as compared to 7,900 in 1946.[21]

The fifties lifestyle placed increased demands on transportation, making the car an indispensable accessory to suburban living. The market for private cars surged dramatically, forcing automobile manufacturers to deliver continuously

figure 5.
Prefab Furniture
Photograph by Tony Venti.

figure 6.
A Week's Work
Nina Leen, *Life* Magazine, © 1947, 1975, Time Inc.

figure 7.
The most noticed little luxury in your home — Soft-Weve
Appears through the courtesy of Scott Paper Company; from the J. Walter Thompson Company Archives.

on their promises of more powerful and flashier models. John B. Rae in *The American Automobile* reported that private automobile registrations in the United States were 25,500,000 when World War II ended. Within the next decade, the figure doubled and by 1960, four-fifths of all American families owned at least one car. As more suburban women assumed the role of family chauffeur, the second car became a necessity, doubling the number of two-car families between 1951 and 1958.[22]

To accommodate this trend and to link suburbs to cities, federal and state governments embarked on colossal road building projects. The cars, in turn, became enormous and showy, with dominant tail lights, jutting fins, and impressive gadgetry. Travelling by car was a firmly established part of national life and recreational enterprises specifically designed for motoring families, such as drive-in movies and roadside motels, enjoyed a booming business.

Madison Avenue understood that Americans were looking for more than technological wizardry when they purchased a Ford, Chrysler or General Motors product. They correctly interpreted and capitalized on an automobile's image-making potential. Through market research, they pinpointed various target audiences and alternately stressed a model's beauty, power, spaciousness or status qualities. It was determined that men and women used a different set of criteria for evaluating a car's value and gender-related advertising became commonplace. Masculine advertisements emphasized a car's horsepower, speed, and technical prowess. Additionally, the automobile was unsurpassed as the ideal male status symbol and ego-enhancing product. In one of their advertising campaigns, Ford introduced their new Thunderbird as a "Mink Coat for Father."

Female-oriented campaigns were powerful reinforcers of the feminine mystique, with constant references to the home and family responsibilities of women. In a 1949 advertisement, a woman from Quincy, Massachusetts offered her testimony that "I taxi my family 25 miles a day . . . so you can guess why I like my new Ford. It feels so safe — something a mother appreciates."[23] That same year *Good Housekeeping* magazine featured an ad with the slogan "A Woman's Place is in the ~~Home~~ Ford." In addition to safety, dependability and convenience, a car's fashionability was a common strategy used to entice the prospective female buyer. The J. Walter Thompson advertising agency reported in their newsletter that "in a unique dealer tie-in and bid for women's attention, Ford is featuring Norris-designed ladies coats in colors to match the New Ford Victorias linking Ford styling with the high fashion trend. The 'Motor Mates.'"[24]

Looking backwards, it is easy to view the mystique as a devious plot and to castigate the women who embraced and were later ensnared by the trap. It is equally tempting to label perpetrators of the myth as the enemy and to denounce all of their manipulative propaganda. This would not only be unfair, it would also be a lie. Men and women were not brainwashed during the 1950s. They were responding to a world deeply shaken by the cataclysmic events of war. It is not difficult to imagine why the image of a secure family life held such appeal to a country forced to suspend this goal during wartime. And if we now see that the means led to damaging ends, we must also recognize that it filled a real need for millions of Americans left frightened and vulnerable by the war.

It would also be inaccurate to state that everyone succumbed to the mystique or that all women had the economic freedom to choose a life at home. Women continued to enter the job market, until by 1960, twice as many women were working as in 1940 and forty percent of all women over sixteen held jobs.[25] What these figures fail to reveal, of course, is that women in the workforce encountered gross forms of discrimination and sex/wage differential. Yet the statistics are important indicators that the feminine mystique was not universally accepted.

From a historical perspective, it is clear that everyone's needs were not the same and the proposed solution was not the anticipated panacea. By the mid-1960s, women, fueled by years of dissatisfaction, were actively seeking change. A revolution was underway. Yet, in the early post-war years, the answers seemed more simple. It is there that women's fashions of the fifties took root.

Women's clothing of the late 1940s and 1950s was more than an aesthetic statement; it was a metaphor of the mystique. As women came to accept their destiny as full-time wives and mothers,

figure 8.

I spend all day cleaning and waxing the floors, then you come home and walk on them.

Cartoon by Hank Ketcham.

figure 9.

Beer belongs . . . enjoy it.

From the J. Walter Thompson Company Archives.

figure 10.

In this friendly, freedom-loving land of ours — beer belongs . . . enjoy it!

From the J. Walter Thompson Company Archives.

fashion supported their response by promoting an idealized vision of passive femininity. Fashion pundits explicitly outlined the accepted formula for a woman's public and private image and pressured women to embrace this visual affirmation of the mystique. The masculine wartime fashions were discordant with the renewed spirit of femininity. The new silhouette replaced the angles with curves and sanctioned the ornamental function of women. As the mystique gathered support, fashions alternately paralleled and promoted the revival of a woman's romanticized identity. It was also a critical corollary to the mystique since women who followed the inflexible fashion prescription were more likely to conform to social expectations. By exaggerating sexual differences and minimizing individual distinctions, feminine self-adornment became an expression of the new mass identity.

> Fashion came out of the first World War with a straight silhouette ... It came out of this war with a waistline.[26]

Just as the feminine myth evolved as a result of the war and its aftermath, so did the fashions of the fifties. Women, tired of five years of fashion isolation and restrictions, became animated by the new post-war spirit. *Harper's Bazaar* informed its readers in 1946 that "you can't be a last-year girl," but change did not occur overnight. Shortages still existed, rationing continued, and the patriotic spirit of austerity lingered; yet an altering of the fashionable shape was definitely set in motion. By adding a few inches of fabric, softening some of the hard edges, and curving in the waistline, designers approved what the rest of the world acknowledged. Men coming out of the trenches were looking for a different kind of woman — not a competitor nor a comrade but a soft, lovely companion. Women were told to reexamine their wartime standards of attractiveness with an eye on the new male perspective.[27] As the feminine look took hold, women began to rediscover their hips, find satisfaction in a small waist, and look twice at their masculine padded shoulders.

This was a period of experimentation for many designers; their 1945-46 collections were eclectic in mood, inspiration, and design. There was a sense that fashion had reached a turning point, but the direction of the change wasn't certain until 1947. During that year, the world received its first look at the work of a man who would dominate fashion for the next ten years — Christian Dior.

With the launching of his Corolle line, which the press dubbed the New Look, Dior became the hero of the day and restored the role of Paris couturier as the most influential force in women's fashion. He accomplished this by correctly intuiting the direction fashion was taking and presenting it to the public as a finished product. In many ways, the New Look was a continuation of the earlier post-war models, yet, where the initial attempts were often tentative and hesitant, Dior's collection telescoped fashion's evolutionary process. The look was polished and perfected and women applauded every line and curve. As Dior explained, "no one person can change fashion — a big fashion change imposes itself. It was because women longed to look like women again that they adopted the New Look ... The change was due to a universal change of feeling, of atmosphere."[28]

The most dramatic feature of the New Look was the length and cut of the skirt. Dior dropped the hemline to twelve to fourteen inches above the floor with a fullness that required as many as twenty-five yards of fabric. Using a flower as inspiration, Dior traced the female figure in cloth to create an exaggerated look of femininity.[29] With his emphasis on a tiny waistline, full hips and swelling breasts, women's erogenous zones were firmly fixed in fashion. These disciplined curves required more than exercise to keep them in shape. Hips and breasts were padded and waist cinchers were revived. Designers began to build these features into their creations and Dior pioneered this new system of dress construction. He devised special boned corsets to cinch in the waist and push up the breasts, and his skirts were shaped with padding, pleats, and stiffened linings. A woman had only to step into a Dior evening gown; the interior scaffolding did the rest.

Although the press lauded Dior and heralded the New Look as a triumphant success, the public had some reservations. Women who admired the longer skirt lengths were suddenly confronted with a closet filled with outdated clothes. Figure 12 shows a model who, after measuring the hemline allowances on all of her dresses, realized that all but four would have to be discarded. Other women were outraged by the cost of a Dior original at a time when victims of the war were starving. Groups of American women banded together to protest the new lengths. When Dior travelled to Dallas to accept an award, he was met by 1,300 members of the Little Below the Knee Club.[30] Not all men found the New Look cause for celebration, either. Dior once received a letter from an angry husband who complained that he couldn't feel his wife through her gown and when he held her it was "like grasping a bird cage."[31]

Yet this was a time when hemline news was headline news and women were eager to express their new feminine identity. Condemnation quickly changed to acceptance and within a year, the universal success of Dior's New Look

figure 11.

The style setter of the '53 season

Appears through the courtesy of Ford Motor Company; from the J. Walter Thompson Company Archives.

figure 12.

Wardrobe Wastage

Jean Speiser, *Life* Magazine, © 1947, 1975, Time Inc.

was an accomplished fact. This influential line would shape women's fashions for the next decade, yet Dior continued to surprise, impress, and delight the public with his artistry in each new collection. By the time of his death in 1958, Dior was selling more than half as much as the rest of the couturiers combined.[32]

In addition to Christian Dior, there was a long list of designers making headline news in the 1950s. Jacques Fath, Pierre Balmain, Madame Grès, Charles James and Lanvin-Castillo topped the list. Women were given another choice when Coco Chanel reopened her salon doors in 1954 after a fifteen year hiatus. Her collection reaffirmed her status as the leader of a special brand of wearable elegance. She represents the important exception to the fashionable rule during the 1950s, for she eschewed any contrivance which deformed the figure or restricted a woman's movement. Although initial press reaction was generally unfavorable, women who prized comfort and classical styling welcomed Chanel back with open arms.

The one designer to rival Dior as the authoritative fashion pace setter was Cristobal Balenciaga. Hailed as the prophet of the silhouette, this Spaniard was a major influence in Paris fashion for several decades. His daytime designs were masterpieces of deceptive simplicity relying on expert cutting and construction for their shape (Photograph 24). Balenciaga's evening gowns were fantasy creations: extravagant, luxurious, and terribly expensive. The results were so unique that Balenciaga stands apart from all other designers. (Color Plate 5).

He loved to design for the mature and hard-to-fit woman, because he believed that the structure of the outfit was more important than the body that it covered. For example, he launched the fashion for three-quarter length sleeves and a distinctive neckline that dipped away from the nape of the neck to draw attention to the parts of a woman's body that remained relatively untouched by the aging process.

Although Balenciaga continued working until his retirement in 1968, he lamented the passing of the fifties as the last great era of the couturier. He believed that the foundation of haute couture rested on the traditional fashion pyramid topped by the privileged elite.[33] As the structure of society shifted during the 1960s and amusement supplanted elegance as the fashionable goal, the unchallenged authority of the couturier came to a halt.

The feminine mystique was based on the principle that women, because of their inherent nature, could be grouped together with little attention paid to individual differences. The same dogmatic approach also applied to the fashions of the period. There was widespread agreement on what was considered appropriate demeanor and appearance. The fashion authorities were executors of the doctrine, and women were taught to accept the rules and follow them religiously. The fashion code dictated that the social occasion would determine a woman's wardrobe choices. For example, a suitable luncheon outfit would be inappropriate for a garden party and a cocktail dress was different from a dinner ensemble. The lines were clearly delineated, and women were never supposed to overstep the boundaries. As a result, the appearance of a fashionable fifties' woman seems studied and self-conscious.

Both dominant silhouettes during the decade were designed to flatter one idealized shape — the hourglass. Full breasts and hips, and a tiny waistline were relentlessly quarried for their appeal; all fashion styles drew attention to these areas. Dior's New Look was the prototype of one silhouette; the other deviated only from the waist down. Instead of the full skirts held in place by layers of crinolines and petticoats (Color Plate 6), the alternate fashion featured a tightly fitting sheath skirt (Photograph 18, Color Plate 7). Reminiscent of the late 1910s' hobble skirt, the pencil-slim sheath immobilized women and further enhanced the passive ideal.[34]

The evening coats of the 1950s provide an interesting contrast to these form-fitting silhouettes. The tent-like coats ballooned out over the figure, their pyramidal shapes providing a perfect foil for the voluptuous curves contained within. Like the stylish dresses and suits, the cut emphasized the soft, sloping shoulder line but they were often hidden by the dramatic sweep of a cape collar (Photograph 20). With deeply pleated panels, full sleeves, and unbroken vertical lines, they were masterpieces of dressmaking (Color Plate 8).

Evening gowns of the period were works of art and artifice. They revealed, yet concealed, a woman's charms, thereby creating an aura of provocative chic. The strapless gown was, by far, the most popular style (see for example Photographs 12 and 13). It not only was responsible for a new appreciation of women's shoulders but it also brought the strapless bra and the merry widow into vogue.[35] Many designers, however, still chose to build the foundation into their creations to ensure that women did not lose in this game of hide-and-seek.

Fabrics used in the construction of these evening gowns were opulent and lavish, often bordering on conspicuous excess. While the new nylon fabrics were favored by many for their uncrushable quality, exclusive haute couture designs often featured silk satins and peau de soie covered with overall patterns of me-

figure 13.

Dior's Rose Pompom Dress
Courtesy *Vogue*, © 1953 (renewed 1981), by The Condé Nast Publications, Inc.

figure 14.

Just a wee bit naughty — but so nice!
Courtesy Warnaco, Inc.

tallic embroidery, beading and sequins (Color Plates 4 and 9). They were all sewn on by hand, so the top designers employed a staff of women whose sole responsibility was the meticulous application of these decorative touches.

No matter how perfect the cut or line of her dress, the picture of the elegant woman was incomplete without the right accessories. The rules of etiquette which governed dress were equally as stringent in determining the proper accoutrements. No detail was too small to escape attention. Gloves came in all lengths to fit every occasion and outfit, umbrellas added a neatly tailored look and jewelry was chosen with utmost care. Handkerchiefs, scarves, and buttonhole flowers were other indispensibles.

Shoes particularly took on a new importance once the New Look arrived. In the delicate balancing of proportions, heels grew higher as women's skirts lengthened. Shoe styling took its directions from the influential fashions, so the delicate shoes of the fifties were the antithesis of the heavy, bulky World War II styles. Once wartime regulations were lifted, women discarded their make-do wooden platforms and cork wedges, and turned instead to elegant leather footwear.[36] As the shoe became more feminine, the styling changed to reveal more of a woman's foot. Worn with the new ultra-sheer nylon stockings, the pointed toes, delicate soles and deeply cut vamps were designed to flatter. The thick, straight heel of the early forties underwent a similar transformation so that by 1953 *Vogue* was urging its readers to think of the new slender heel as "the

stem of a champagne glass." The trend continued until it peaked in the mid-1950s with the stiletto heel. Originating in Italy, this style featured an extremely high and narrow heel that was the ruination of floors and carpets.[37] Perched on top of their three to four inch heels, women no longer walked; they teetered. These sophisticated, distorting, and irrational shoes provide an emphatic visual notation of the feminine mystique.

During the second half of the decade, the fashion pendulum reversed its direction as shoe styles changed in unison with the clothes. As skirt lengths began to inch upwards and more of a woman's leg was revealed, the arched sophistication of the stiletto heel diminished in importance. Heels became lower, exaggerated points were softened or cut off entirely, and casual shoes and sandals gained in popularity. This mood towards more functional footwear would eventually pave the way for the boot explosion of the 1960s[38] (Photograph 30).

Throughout the 1940s, it was unthinkable for a woman to go out of doors without a hat. The rules eased somewhat during the course of the 1950s, but fashion etiquette still decreed that for formal occasions, a hat was de rigeur. Hats were an essential part of the total fashion picture, so women carefully coordinated their hats to complement their clothes and other accessories. Similar to couture dress designs, couture millinery set the trends for new fashions and the mass market followed suit (Photograph 28). Sizes, shapes and styles varied considerably, ranging from the extrava-

gantly romantic to the neatly tailored. Some of the more popular styles were the boater, pillbox, cartwheel, beret, and souwester, a favorite of Dior.[39] A wide variety of materials appeared, including straw, velours, and felt for daytime wear. Evening styles often incorporated silk, satin, jewels, and feathers. Veiling was used to lend an unmistakable air of mystery to a woman's appearance.

To accommodate the growing trend toward casual apparel, women often chose headscarves as their fashion accessory. This style began during the war years as a protective head covering for factory workers and a cover-up for women who needed to camouflage the fact that a daily shampoo was a pre-war luxury. Yet once the war ended, the scarf was revived for its decorative appeal.[40] The fashion continued to be worn throughout the 1950s and into the sixties. It provided the perfect answer for the woman who did not wish to abandon the practice of wearing a hat but balked at the rigid formality of many of the popular styles.

In the early years of the decade, hairstyles were determined by the shape of the hat. Women commonly wore their hair combed away from the face and pinned or rolled into a neat chignon. As the decade advanced and women began to experiment with fuller hairstyles, hats became an encumbrance. Instead of changing their coiffures, women began to discard their hats. This was particularly true for the bouffant and beehive hair-dos. These towering edifices, which depended on heavy teasing and sometimes false hair for their exagger-

figure 15.
The shorter your sleeves, the longer your gloves
Van Raalte Gloves, Division of Honey Fashions, photo courtesy *Life* Magazine

figure 16.
Rafia Accessories
Courtesy *Vogue*, © 1944 (renewed 1972), by The Condé Nast Publications, Inc.

figure 17.
How to be a Blonde!
Courtesy of Helena Rubinstein, Inc.

ated height, were heavily lacquered to keep every sticky hair in place. At first favored by younger women, the styles gained widespread favor, much to the milliners' dismay.[41]

The image of beauty during the 1950s was rigidly fixed in the public's mind and woman's compliance was an essential corollary to the mystique. At a time when a woman's external appearance often determined her popularity, the dictates of fashion exerted rigid rules which became a measuring stick for her acceptance. Yet if, as Alison Lurie proposes, clothing does have its own language, the message of fifties' fashions is a mixed one.[42] Indeed, the same tensions which characterized societal attitudes towards women also typify the period's dress. The ambiguities of the period's dress invested women with two very different personae: dutiful homemaker and tempting siren. The former wore the shirtwaist dress, apron, and demure necklines — all proper symbols of domesticity. Yet, at the same time, an exaggerated image of sexuality prevailed. Woman-turned-temptress titilated her man with plunging necklines, veiled eyes and a come-hither walk. Fashion encouraged women to become chameleon-like characters, shifting effortlessly from wholesome homemaker to wanton lover with a change of clothes. Nowhere is this dichotomous approach to the fantasy woman more obvious than in the decade's choice of movie stars.

Beginning with the initial popularity of the movies in the 1910s, film stars have been defined by and have influenced prevailing definitions of the 20th century American beauty. The public seized upon Hollywood goddesses for models of glamour and allure yet their choice of film idols was based heavily on contemporary values. For example, Katherine Hepburn, Joan Crawford and other feisty career women of the late 1930s projected an image of confidence and independence. Even though a happy ending still meant marriage, the assertive nature of the heroine showed through. However, after the war, instead of following the further escapades of Rosie the Riveter, new types of film stars emerged who embodied the spirit of the feminine mystique.

During the 1950s, female stars tended to fall into one of two categories. There were the so-called mammary goddesses, such as Jane Russell, Lana Turner, and Ava Gardner, whose voluptuous curves and sultry glances promised sexual pleasures. This type was balanced by the girl-next-door typified by Doris Day, America's freshly scrubbed, ever cheerful homemaker. Lois Banner, in *American Beauty* heralds Marilyn Monroe as the most important female film representative of the 1950s, based on her ability to combine both characterizations with her special brand of innocent sexuality.[43]

Movie stars not only influenced standards of beauty; they also introduced new fashion trends with their on- and off-screen costumes.[44] Stars captured the public's imagination with their expensive homes, non-conforming lifestyles, and well-publicized affairs and divorces. It was a curious twist to the American dream, and the public devoured every bit of information that publicists and gossip columnists threw its way.

This was the last great era of movie star idolatry on a large scale. As more and more people turned on their television sets, movie attendance dropped off and rising costs sharply curtailed the production of sweeping movie spectacles. As budgetary constraints increased, costume departments were one of the first expenses to be cut. Directors sought out less expensive locations, new independent film makers, and the Hollywood mystique began to fade.[45] Additionally, the new crop of stars rebelled against studio-manipulated careers and refused to build their lives around a predetermined image. As the changes occurred, the lavish costumes of earlier years became anachronistic. The bugle beads, sequins and furs were relegated to storage and the Hollywood-inspired wardrobe became obsolete.

However, during its prime, Hollywood was a potent force in shaping the iconic imagery of the mystique. Women everywhere tried to imitate the stars, often relying on artificial means to achieve that special brand of glamour. When it appeared that blondes did indeed have more fun, sales of peroxide skyrocketed. And when fans were busy memorizing the measurements of their favorite "sweater girl," women worked to improve their own vital statistics. Although special exercises, creams, and bust-improving gadgets were on the market, the exaggerated Hollywood cleavage demanded special brassieres. With their padding, wiring, stiffening and circular stitching, they truly earned the name

figure 18.
I dreamed I was a toreador in my Maidenform bra.
Courtesy of Maidenform, Inc.

figure 19.
Revlon's Fire and Ice
Courtesy Revlon.

foundation garments.[46] The resulting uplifted shape bore little resemblance to a woman's natural form. Breasts became rigid appurtenances that were independent of the rest of the body.

In addition to the guiding force of movie stars, cosmetics companies exerted a power over the course of fashion by peddling their own brand of commercial beauty. Make-up was considered an indispensible part of the fifties' face and, like fashionable dress, cosmetics exaggerated a woman's features. For women who were inculcated with the importance of one's appearance, to go without make-up was to feel undressed. The two dominant facial areas were the lips and eyes, and both were treated to lavish attention. The elaborate artifice required time, skill, and a sizeable investment. To create the nighttime look, beauty editors advised the use of moisture cream, tinted foundation, and heavy powder as well as eyeshadow, eyebrow pencil, eyeliner, mascara, lipstick, and false eyelashes. Curves were dominant and outlining was used to extend the shape of the lips and eyes. As veiled hats gained in popularity, women became even more heavy-handed in the application of cosmetics to ensure that their features would be visible through the netting (veiling also made long cigarette holders an indispensible prop).[47]

In the highly competitive cosmetics field, advertising plays a crucial role. During the 1950s many companies used the endorsement of Hollywood stars to promote their products. Others relied heavily on a sexual lure, with the dichotomy of the American woman as good girl/bad girl forming the basis of many successful marketing strategies. Charles Revson pioneered the trend in 1952 when he introduced his "Fire and Ice" campaign. Women were encouraged to acknowledge and express their hidden sensual personality by using "Fire and Ice" cosmetics. Other firms quickly followed suit and cosmetics advertising became progressively more sexually explicit as the decade advanced.[48]

If it is indeed possible to generalize about fashionable stereotypes of the 1950s, it is also important to note the variations. Although the dominant silhouette rooted in the couture tradition prevailed, distinctions were made often based on a woman's age and lifestyle. For example, the multiplicity of roles and the home orientation of the suburban housewife necessitated an approach to fashion that was different from that of the well-to-do society matron. A casual style arose from the suburban milieu, and the important innovators of this mode were American designers.

The rising prominence of the American fashion industry accelerated as a result of World War II. Although some of the Parisian houses remained open during the Occupation, the Germans halted all of their export business. Faced with this silence from abroad, America looked towards its native talent for fashion direction. U.S. designers were able to quickly respond to the challenge for two reasons. First, wartime restrictions and regulations were implemented later and lasted for a shorter period of time in this country than they did in Europe.[49] Second, American designers were able to capitalize on the fact that the United States was leading the rest of the world in mass production techniques. Drawing on these strengths, designers such as Claire McCardell and Hattie Carnegie (Photograph 19) gained world-wide attention and recognition. Their informal separates and coordinates became an American trademark.

A Gimbel's advertisement that appeared in the *New York Times* in 1954 proclaimed that "The New Good Life is casual, defrilled, comfortable, fun and isn't it marvelous." This was the suburban dream, the shirtwaist dress its uniform. Women loved the style because it was flattering, moderately priced and it did not become out-moded with a designer's seasonal whims. Since the shirtwaister did not demand rigid underpinnings, it was easy to wear and the small collars, pastel colors, and tiny floral prints created a feeling that was inherently feminine. The increased use of synthetic fabrics, such as the nylon petticoats and permanently pleated cloths, offered added convenience and gave the dress a lasting look of precise neatness. Additionally, the shirtwaist closely followed the fashionable silhouette with its well-defined waistline, fitted bodice, and billowing skirts, making it the perfect choice for the busy homemaker.

As the suburban family spent more of its leisure hours out of doors, entertaining styles relaxed. The new informality demanded a special wardrobe of play clothes. Halter-style dresses, bared midriffs and dirndl skirts all appeared in brilliant colors.[50] As more occasions war-

figure 20.

Shirtwaist Dress

William Helburn, Life, Magazine, © 1954, 1982, Time, Inc.

figure 21.

Play clothes for leisure . . .

Reprinted with permission of *Travel-Holiday*, Travel Building, Floral Park, New York.

figure 22.

No wonder she's so well dressed. She has three big brothers.

Cartoon by William Von Riegen.

ranted active sportswear, American designers were inspired to feature a wide variety of slack styles ranging from the pedal-pusher to the slack suit. For general use, however, pants, jeans, and shorts were the perogative of youth during the 1950s.

Age began to play an increasingly important role in determining a woman's clothing choices as the decade advanced. By the mid-1950s, there was a growing movement that began to vie for attention with the predominant ideal of the mature, sophisticated woman. Set apart by a generation gap, the teenager emerged as an important trend setter. Suddenly, to be young was to be special. The children of the baby boom were growing up with money in their pockets and a desire to spend, spend, spend.

Recognizing the importance of this highly lucrative market, advertisers and manufacturers began to capitalize on the ever-changing fads and customs of the nation's youth. *Vogue* formally acknowledged the separate identity of this market when it introduced its "Young Idea" feature in 1952 which was aimed at the 17-25 age group.[51] Soon, specialized magazines devoted exclusively to a young clientele flooded the market. This newfound identity brought with it a growing sense of self-sufficiency. The spirit of the fifties teenager continued to gain momentum and eventually culminated in the sixties revolution with the assertion of the adolescent.

The progression of the change was spasmodic. The youth of the 1950s were, in many ways, extensions of their parents. For the vast majority, security still meant marriage. These young adults were not ready to denounce the principles of the conservative mystique.[52] Conforming to peer pressures often conflicted with the canons of respectable behavior; the clothing of the fifties teenager records this identity struggle. Ponytails, jeans, bobby socks, dirndl skirts and coordinated sweater sets were the distinctive garb of the girls during the daytime. Yet at night, they turned into junior replicas of their mothers with their strapless gowns, glove-encased arms and well-groomed coiffures.

Gradually, the balance of fashion leadership shifted with the growing social, political, and economic power of the nation's youth. As the tension heightened, women's appearance began to visibly change. The hourglass shape deflated into a cylinder, sophistication was abandoned for frivolity, and repression gave way to permissiveness as the mystique lost its hold. During the late 1950s, a new transitional silhouette dominated the fashion scene. The sack dress, or chemise, with its straight lines and low slung belt, altered the direction of fashion and eased the way for the simple A-line dresses of the sixties (Photographs 26 and 27). The hemline began its inexorable move upwards during these years, so that by 1963, a woman's knees were exposed. Two years later, skirts barely covered the thigh.

The rising importance of the teenager marked the end for the celebrated mature woman of the 1950s. In their efforts to emulate the new standard of beauty, i.e. a narrow, underdeveloped body, women seemed to shrink in size. And where previously they had tried to maintain a perennial age of 35, 25 became the crucial cut-off point. The eccentricities of youth became the new target of exploitation.

Significantly, the change coincided with a decline in the supremacy of the feminine mystique. By the early 1960s, many women were no longer willing to ignore their frustration with the domestic ideal. As their vexation grew, they stopped listening to the oracles of the feminine doctrine and started to heed their own inner voices. They also began to join forces. Women, who ten years earlier had rejected any hint of organized feminism, were banding together in protest. This was only one step in a much larger revolution, yet, it was an important beginning.[53] It encouraged women to adjust their life plans and helped to make the sex-role stereotyping engendered by the mystique obsolete. In the process, women rebelled against the fashions which incarnated the mythic situation of the fifties' woman by reveling in her domesticity.

The search for outward visible signs of a new sense of purpose and freedom typifies the spirit of the sixties. The fashion descriptor of the decade was "liberated" and it altered all previous norms. The new wave of design innovators rejected the styles which showed off a woman's natural, and not so natural, curves to full advantage. Instead, they chose stark, geometric lines to accentuate the new boyish shape.[54] The results were often transitory fads; however, this climate of experimentation brought about a lasting change. During the 1950s, the couture establishment sanctioned an extremely narrow definition of what was "in fashion" and total compliance to the rigid standardization was expected. As more and more of these rules were shattered in the sixties, a greater sense of freedom emerged.[55] The concept of fashion and its vocabulary expanded to include a wide variety of styles, looks and tastes.

It is clear that from 1945 to 1965, images of women shifted dramatically. The quintessential lady, imperatively feminine and carefully constructed, no longer had a place in the new social ethic of the 1960s. Women began to consciously and unconsciously realize that, although the clothing of the 1950s did not invent the mystique, it certainly helped to cement women in that role.

figure 23.

Big night . . . snapshot night!

Appears through the courtesy of Eastman Kodak Company; from the J. Walter Thompson Company Archives.

figure 24.

Haircut by Vidal Sassoon

Courtesy *Vogue*, © 1963 by The Condé Nast Publications, Inc.

And individuals, weary of heeding fashion's injunctions, were no longer willing to judge social desirability solely on the basis of appropriate dress. The trappings of the happy housewife were perceived as exploitive ornamentation and the fashions which hinted at sexual seductiveness were superfluous to young women trying to be frankly uninhibited. By rejecting the fashionable imagery, women were repudiating the underlying message as well, and clothing, which had once symbolized women's obedient acceptance of the passive role, evolved into one of their strongest forms of protest.

Notes

[1] Christian Dior, *Christian Dior and I*, trans. Antonio Fraser, (New York, 1957), p. 35.

[2] This phrase was first coined by Betty Friedan in 1963 to describe the mythic situation of the middle-class housewife-mother in America. Her critique of sex-role expectations sparked a revolutionary change in attitude and provided women with a philosophical justification to seek fulfillment outside of the home.

[3] Agnes Meyer, "Women Aren't Men," *Atlantic*, 186, No. 2, August, 1950, p. 33.

[4] Barbara Heggie, "Back on the Pedestal, Ladies," *Vogue*, 107, No. 2, January 15, 1946, p. 118.

[5] Marynia Farnham and Ferdinand Lundberg, *Modern Woman: The Lost Sex*, (New York, 1947). See also Betty Friedan, *The Feminine Mystique*, (New York, 1963), pp. 119-20 for her analysis of this work.

[6] William Chafe, *The American Woman*, (New York, 1972), pp. 199-210.

[7] Friedan, *Mystique*, particularly Chapter 1, "The Problem That Has No Name," pp. 11-27.

[8] Landon Jones, *Great Expectation*, (New York, 1980), pp. 19-35. Jones notes that the euphoria of the baby boom was a national phenomenon, affecting all classes and races.

[9] Ibid., p. 2.

[10] Philip Slater, *The Pursuit of Loneliness*, (Boston, 1970), p. 67.

[11] Douglas T. Miller and Marion Novak, *The Fifties*, (New York, 1977), pp. 132-39.

[12] William Whyte, Jr., *The Organization Man* (New York, 1956), presents a portrait of the new breed of young executives in the 1950's who believed in the sense of belonging as the ultimate need of the individual. For an analysis of the corporate wife, see William Whyte, Jr., "The Wives of Management," *Fortune*, October, 1951, pp. 86-87.

[13] Park Forest Homes, Inc., November 19, 1952.

[14] Magazines from the fifties are filled with do-it-yourself projects, instructions and kits for the entire family.

[15] For a discussion of the fashionable image of the 19th century woman, see Barbara Welter, "The Cult of True Womanhood: 1820-1860," in *Our American Sisters: Women in American Life and Thought* ed., Jean E. Friedman and William G. Shade (Boston, 1973).

[16] Meyer, "Women Aren't Men," p. 35.

[17] For a history of American housework and its relationship to the American housewife, see Susan Strasser, *Never Done*, (New York, 1982).

[18] See Friedan, *Mystique*, pp. 197-223 for her discussion of motivational researchers and the role of American women as victims in the advertising game.

[19] John Brooks, *The Great Leap*, (New York, 1966), pp. 161-165 and Whitney Stine "Early Television: Kingdom of Shadows," in *The Human Side of History* ed., Raymond Locke, (Los Angeles, 1970), pp. 248-49.

[20] Martin Mayer, "Television's Lords of Creations," *Harper's*, 213, No. 1278, November, 1956, p. 25.

[21] Miller and Novak, *The Fifties*, p. 7.

[22] John B. Rae, *The American Automobile*, (Chicago, 1966), pp. 92-95, 192-94.

[23] "Out Front with All America," Ford advertisement, *Farm Journal*, 1949.

[24] *J. Walter Thompson Company News*, VII, No. 6, November 17, 1952.

[25] William Chafe, *The American Woman, 1920-1970*, (New York, 1972), p. 218.

[26] "The Day Before Spring," *Harper's Bazaar*, LXXX, No. 3, March, 1946, p. 13.

[27] Dorothy Kay Thompson, "The New Spirit," *Harper's Bazaar*, LXXX, No. 4, April, 1946, p. 123.

[28] Christian Dior, *Talking About Fashion*, (New York, 1954), p. 23.

[29] For a biographical account of Dior's life and his achievements as a designer, see Brigid Keenan, *Dior in Vogue*, (New York, 1981).

[30] Jane Dorner, *Fashions in the Forties and Fifties*, (New York, 1975), p. 9.

[31] Richard Donovan, "That Friend of Your Wife's Named Dior," *Collier's*, 135, No. 12, June 10, 1955, p. 35.

[32] Madge Garland, *Fashion*, (Harmondsworth, England, 1962), p. 41.

[33] Kennedy Fraser, *The Fashionable Mind*, (New York, 1981), pp. 73-89.

[34] Introduced by Paul Poiret, the hobble skirt had a wide band encircling it just below the knees which forced women to take short, mincing steps when they walked. See Lois Banner, *American Beauty*, (New York, 1982), for an analysis of the relationship between fashion and the image of feminine beauty.

[35] The merry widow was a combination half-bra, corset, and garter foundation garment. Elizabeth Ewing presents a history of underwear as part of the fashion and social process in *Dress and Undress*, (New York, 1978).

[36] For a discussion of wartime rationing and clothing by government decree see Georgina Howell, *In Vogue*, (New York, 1978) pp. 157-66, and Julian Robinson, *Fashion in the Forties*, (New York, 1976).

[37] Ernestine Carter, *The Changing World of Fashion*, (New York, 1977), p. 203.

[38] Christina Probert, *Shoes in Vogue*, (New York, 1981), pp. 52-53, 62-63.

[39] Christina Probert, *Hats in Vogue*, (New York, 1981), pp. 44-45, 58-59.

[40] Elizabeth Ewing, *History of 20th Century Fashion*, Second Edition, (London, 1975), p. 144.

[41] Carter, *The Changing World*, pp. 198-99.

[42] Alison Lurie, *The Language of Clothes*, (New York, 1981).

[43] Banner, *American Beauty*, pp. 278-286.

[44] Brigid Keenan, *The Women We Wanted to Look Like*, (New York, 1977), pp. 75-87.

[45] Miller and Novak, *The Fifties*, pp. 314-330. A history of Hollywood's contribution to twentieth century fashion is presented by W. Robert Lavine in *In A Glamorous Fashion*, (New York, 1980).

[46] Howell, *In Vogue*, p. 207, cites the popular fifties' dormitory chant, "I must, I must, achieve a bigger bust. I will, I will, make it bigger still. Hoorah, hoorah, I need a bigger bra."

[47] Ibid., p. 242.

[48] Banner, *American Beauty*, pp. 271-274.

[49] Ewing, *History of 20th Century Fashion*, pp. 147-48.

[50] Tony Robin, "America's Own Fashions," *Holiday*, 12, No. 1, July, 1952, pp. 102-107.

[51] Dorner, *Fashions in the Forties and Fifties*, p. 48.

[52] Miller and Novak, *The Fifties*, pp. 268-277.

[53] See chapter 14, "A New Life Plan For Women," in Friedan, *Mystique*.

[54] Barbara Bernard, *Fashion in the 60's*, (New York, 1978), p. 32.

[55] Banner, *American Beauty*, p. 290.

Photograph 1
Two-piece Suit
Adrian
circa 1942

As one of America's best known film costume designers during the 1930s and 1940s, Adrian dressed the most popular stars, including Joan Crawford, Greta Garbo, and Jean Harlow. This was a time when knowing eyes looked to Hollywood stars' off-screen and on-screen wardrobes for fashion directives and Adrian helped to shape the taste of American women. He expanded his influence when, in 1942, he opened the doors to his own salon. Adrian's flair for the dramatic coupled with his distinctive workmanship made his creations the popular choice for thousands of women. This suit, with its narrow skirt, masculine styling, and exaggerated padded shoulders, illustrates his trademark — the coat hanger silhouette.

Photograph 2
Cocktail Dress
Nat Tuman, New York
circa 1940-42

The occupation of France in 1941 necessitated a change in fashion leadership. Cut off from Paris couture, American designers and manufacturers began to draw on native talent for their inspiration. However, by 1942, in addition to coping with material shortages, American designers had to comply with the Government Order L85. This legislation set limits on yardage allotments as well as prohibited superfluous details and fabric-wasting fashions (such as the dolman sleeves and skirt flounces on this dress). As a result, restrained austerity became the new design yardstick and the squared-shoulder silhouette with the accompanying narrow, short skirt became the feminine wartime uniform.

Photograph 3
Two-piece Suit
D. Veltry, New York
circa 1944

Tailored suits were the preferred choice for many women during the war. They could carry a woman from daytime to evening with a change of accessories and their mix-and-match potential expanded a woman's wardrobe. Although materials grew more scarce, hats were not restricted or rationed by government decree. They provided fanciful relief for women obliged to forego other luxuries, such as sheer silk stockings or a new dress. Typical of the early 1940s' styles, this hat is designed to be worn slightly tilted and perched low over the forehead.

Photograph 4

Day Dress and Jacket
Milgrim
circa 1944

The masculine silhouettes of the war years were often softened by expert styling. In this ensemble, the jacket sleeves
and bodice are cut from one piece to round the shoulder line.
The severity of the skirt line is relieved by horizontal hipline
pleating, and the dress yoke and jacket lining provide contrast
to the uniformity of the design. The stringencies of war and
government restrictions forced designers to eliminate frills and
concentrate, instead, on function. Extravagance was demodé,
simplicity was in.

Photographs 5 and 6

Day Dress and Jacket — Detail
Milgrim
circa 1944

The cut of a dress or suit assumed new importance during the war years. These two close-ups show innovations in cut and design. The jacket back extension and bodice are constructed to give the illusion of a yoke and collar. Self-fabric bias trim is skillfully applied to the dress bodice to add a decorative touch.

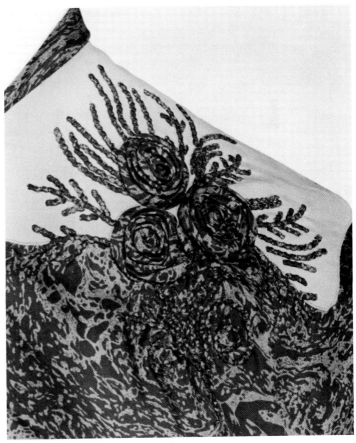

Photograph 7

Evening Gown
Bergdorf Goodman label
sold 1-25-46

The immediate post-war period saw no new dramatic silhouette. Recovery was slow; austerity was still a primary concern. There was a general softening of the line and a sparked interest in femininity but it would take several years before new directions would be firmly established. This gown illustrates the mood of the transition years. The broad shoulder look prevails but the silhouette is softened by the shirred bodice and gathered waistline. The choice of nylon fabric is also typical of this period. The synthetic fiber, developed by DuPont scientists, was commercially introduced at the end of the 1930s. Once the government recognized the extensive capabilities of this fiber, most of the available nylon went to the war effort. It was not until the end of the war that civilians had a readily available supply at their disposal.

Photograph 8

Evening Coat
Elizabeth Arden, New York design by Castillo
circa 1947

In 1944, Elizabeth Arden, noted manufacturer of cosmetics and missonary of beauty, opened a fashion department at her Fifth Avenue salon. The following year she persuaded Antonio Castillo to come to the United States from Paris to design for her. He stayed for five years and created approximately nine collections of custom and ready-made clothing. In 1950, Castillo returned to Paris and joined the staff of La Maison Jeanne Lanvin. The *New York Times* reporter Barbara Pope, commenting on Castillo's second collection for Elizabeth Arden, wrote that "he dares to venture into new forms and . . . yet he never loses sight of the fashion importance of the feminine figure."

Photograph 9

Dress and Jacket (left)
Castillo for Elizabeth Arden
1947

Coat (right)
Elizabeth Arden, New York
circa 1951

Fabrics are as much a part of fashion as the variations in a silhouette. Dior once commented, "Fabric not only expresses a designer's dreams but also stimulates his own ideas. It can be the beginning of an inspiration." The polka dot fabric of this Castillo design represents a highly complex and sophisticated technology. The fact that the fabric was copyrighted in 1947 is testimony to its uniqueness (copyright information is stamped on the selvage). The discharge printing consisted of dyeing the fabric in a solid medium blue color. Then, instead of printing the white dots with a pigment, the white areas were treated with a bleach to remove, or discharge, the blue color. A navy pigment was then printed onto the fabric to outline and define the white polka dots.

Photograph 10
Two-piece Suit
D. Veltry
circa 1950-53

While it is true that the New Look caused a sensation when it was introduced in 1947, it did not meet with universal approval. Women in the United States joined together in protest to form "A Little Below the Knee Club." Other women chose to incorporate only elements of the new style. This suit combines the nipped-in waist, bias skirt and gentle shaping of the more feminine silhouette with the masculine tailoring of earlier styles.

Photograph 11

Strapless Evening Gown
Bergdorf Goodman label
sold 1-12-51

The figure-revealing styles of the 1950s demanded a slim body and a narrow waist. Many women needed a little help in achieving the hour-glass figure; sales of foundationwear soared during the period. Corsets, girdles, stiffened petticoats, and padded bras all were used to give Nature a helping hand. The popularity of strapless dresses demanded the development of the strapless bra. Designed to push-up and accentuate the bust line, they often were wired underneath the bust to produce the exaggerated bosom so admired in the fifties.

Photograph 12
Strapless Evening Gown
Bergdorf Goodman label
sold 1-12-51

The unusually intricate workmanship on the gown skirt is typical of the period's attention to detail. The trapunto decoration was applied by hand with wrapped metallic yarns. The process consists of sewing two pieces of fabric (in this case, the outer skirt and muslin lining) using very tiny quilting stitches. Small tufts of padding are then pushed into the outlined areas with a needle or sharp instrument to create a raised, three-dimensional design. The same trapunto technique was used to decorate quilt tops and counterpanes in 18th and 19th century America.

Photograph 13
Strapless Evening Gown
Bergdorf Goodman label
sold 1-12-51

Couturiers selected their fabrics carefully, often commissioning special fabrics to complement their designs. Selecting the expensive velvets, silks, and taffetas was an integral part of the process and served to separate the cheap imitation from its haute couture prototype. The harmony of the amethyst silk faille and slate grey peau de soie in this gown accentuates the gracefulness of the silhouette. Pleated sections of the curved bodice cross diagonally and four panels of varying length cascade over the petal skirt.

Photograph 14

Strapless Evening Gown and Shoulder Wrap
Bergdorf Goodman label
sold 1-12-51

Evening fashions of the 1950s are striking in their elegance
and sophistication. Yet, the appearance of a woman's "natural
beauty" was often based on an elaborately constructed artifice. Built-in shaping and foundation garments assisted in
promoting the seductive charms of the fairer sex. This cam-
ouflaged perfection of form epitomized the decorative ideal
of women during the decade.

Photograph 15
Bodice and Skirt
Christian Dior
1954

Fashion reporters used to comment that Dior created shapes that could walk across the room alone. In addition to his complex system of inner shaping, Dior relied on stiff fabrics as in this matching bodice and skirt. Distributing weights along the hemline ensured that the new short skirt silhouette would hang correctly at all times. Note the center back button closure; it was a favorite Dior device.

Photograph 16
Jacket and Skirt
Christian Dior
1954

Dior's Spring/Summer collection of 1954 has been hailed as one of his loveliest lines. He called it "Lily of the Valley" which was his lucky flower and the clothes were youthful and pretty. One of his favorite themes that season was the sailor look; boaters, sailor hats, and blouson battledress tops were seen again and again. In this outfit, Dior used the shaping and knotwork of the sailor tie in the design of the attached waistline sash.

Photograph 17
Cocktail Dress
circa 1950-55

Although not every woman could afford an exclusive designer creation fit to her specifications, she could still remain in fashion. Some designers featured their own ready-to-wear boutiques which promised substantial savings. The majority of women, however, depended on mass-produced clothing to fill out their wardrobe. Major department stores and manufacturers could order several models from the couture houses with a license to mass produce them. Other clothing firms simply took their directions from the latest collections to produce a line that captured the spirit of couture. This off-the-rack dress follows the ultra-feminine styling of its designer counterpart.

Photograph 18
Afternoon Dress
circa 1955

Although the full skirts of the New Look persisted in their appeal throughout the 1950s, fashion accommodated an alternate shape — the straight, sheath skirt. The silhouette was hard to wear since it revealed every figure flaw; it flattered only the slender woman. It was also a restrictive style. The narrow hemline made walking difficult and forced women to adopt a decorative, non-functional pose. This dress, with its tight-fitting sleeves, body hugging skirt, and bustle silhouette bears a striking resemblance to the bustle dress of the 1870s. Like its Victorian predecessor, inner skirt tapes are attached to this dress to secure the bustle flounce.

Photograph 19
Cocktail Dress
Hattie Carnegie
circa 1953-55

Hattie Carnegie began her career as a messenger girl at Macy's in the early 1900s. In 1909, she opened her first mil-linery boutique and from there she expanded her business to include women's clothing of her own design. Her success continued to grow until by 1949, her wholesale and retail shops were doing an eight million dollar a year business. Her exclusive designs tended to be luxurious but conventional and appealed to the American taste. She was a favorite designer of the actress Gertrude Lawrence who wore Carnegie crea-tions in all of her American plays.

Photograph 20
Evening Coat
Balenciaga
circa 1950-55

This coat illustrates the dramatic style of Cristobel Balenciaga. The shape of the enveloping coat is deceptively simple; it could be achieved only by expert cutting and calculated seaming. The sweeping cape collar which frames the face and the full shorter sleeves are part of Balenciaga's legacy to the world of fashion.

Photograph 21
Coat
Christian Dior
1955

As teenagers began to establish their separate identity during the 1950s, they opened up a whole new category of the fashion market. The youthful impulse behind the bobby socks, jeans, and ponytails began to infiltrate the world of high fashion and astute designers sought to incorporate a portion of the new spirit in their collections. The youthful styling of this coat exemplifies this trend. It has the ease and freedom desired by youth combined with Dior's characteristic attention to defined shape and detail.

Photograph 22
Strapless Gown
Christian Dior
1956

Each season, Dior chose a new theme for his collection. For three of his more controversial lines, Dior looked to the alphabet for inspiration. In his H, Y and A lines, Dior's aim was to change the proportions of a woman's body to approximate the shape of the designated letter. In his H line, for example, he pushed the bust upwards, dropped the waist, and accentuated the hipline (to form the crossbar of the H). In the autumn of 1956, Dior showed a return to romantic prettiness as shown in this delicately embroidered velvet evening gown.

Photograph 23
Strapless Gown
Christian Dior
1959

During the 1950s, Paris haute couture was essentially a hand-craft industry. Individual fittings, intricate tailoring, and hand-sewn decoration were all the work of behind-the-scene seam-stresses who meticulously turned the designer's sketch into a finished product. They would begin by interpreting the sketch and creating a muslin pattern (toile). Initially draped and fitted on a dummy, they were later modelled by live mannequins for the designer's approval, alterations, or rejection. Couturiers took great pride in their highly personal service which distin-guished their work from the assembly line world of ready-to-wear. Dior explained: "In a machine age, dressmaking is one of the last refuges of the human, the personal, the inimitable." This gown is a testimony to that personal service. A profusion of clear beads, silver sequins and pailletes, and rhinestones were individually sewn on by hand. Several layers of the five layer skirt were decorated in this manner to ensure an overall effect of luxurious glitter.

Photograph 24
Three-piece Suit
Balenciaga
1963

Balenciaga approached the cut of clothes in a highly unique
fashion. Designed for the mature and often hard-to-fit woman,
they were meant to flatter. His creations have often been
described as timeless and it was this insurance of longevity
that appealed to many of his clients. His innovations appear
over and over again. For example, the free-flowing lines, lower
cut neckline, and slightly wider armseye that Balenciaga popularized during the 1950s are updated in this 1963 suit. Weights
are attached to the back jacket lining to maintain the ease of
the blouson styling.

Photograph 25
Evening Gown
Courrèges
circa 1963

Unlike the designers of the 1950s who tried to achieve a balance between the parts of a garment and the accessories, designers of the 1960s concerned themselves with the proportions of the dress and the amount of skin bared. Particularly obvious in the mini-skirted styles, it was also true for evening wear. This gown flaunts the bare arm which has been stripped of its long glove. Curves are gone; they are replaced with angles. Courrèges carries through with this theme in his choice of geometric vinyl appliques.

Photograph 26
Dress
Yves Saint Laurent
1966

At the age of 21, Yves Saint Laurent succeeded Christian Dior as head designer of the House of Dior. For his first collection, he created the highly successful trapeze shape which hung freely from the wearer's shoulders. This line foreshadowed Saint Laurent's major strength as a designer. In 1961, he established his own salon and throughout the decade, he produced silhouettes well-known for their exacting cut and precision of line. This A-line dress achieves its gentle shaping from the woman's body as opposed to the rigid structures of the 1950s that imposed their own shape. The dropped waistline elongates the line and constrasts sharply with the waist-cinching styles of the previous decade.

Photograph 27
Dress
Yves Saint Laurent
circa 1965

 The revolution against established patterns which typifies the mood of the sixties' fashion world led to a vogue for ethnic fashions. While youth wholeheartedly adopted the traditional garb of almost every country, designers began incorporating elements of ethnic clothing into their collections. Yves Saint Laurent drew upon African prints for inspiration to create this mini-skirted dress. His stylized version of a ritual collar includes a wide variety of colored wooden, glass and plastic beads decorated with multi-colored embroidery stitches.

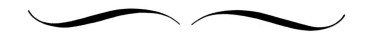

Photograph 28

Hat (top left)
Balenciaga
circa 1956-60

Hat (top right)
Florence Wilson Norfolk
circa 1949-54

Hat (center left)
Schiaparelli
circa 1953-56

Hat (center right)
Florence Wilson Norfolk
circa 1947-53

Hat (bottom left)
Milgrim
Florence Wilson Norfolk
circa 1950-55

Hat (bottom right)
Strictly from Unger New York
circa 1955-59

By 1960, hats were no longer considered an essential accessory but during the early and mid-1950s they reigned supreme. Hats not only were selected carefully to complement the clothing, but women often built an entire outfit around the design of a hat. They were so important that women's hairstyles were shaped to accommodate the style of a hat. Milliners showed remarkable skill in creating new and exciting designs each season. Since different occasions demanded different hat styles, fabrics and colors, the fashion conscious women's closet often resembled a small milliner's shop.

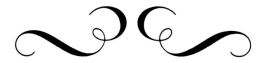

Photograph 29
(from left to right)

Shoe
Florsheim
circa 1940-45

Shoe
Massaro Opera
circa 1949-54

Shoe
Designer Originals Jacqueline
circa 1950-55

Shoe
Hofheimer's Cavalier deLuxe
circa 1955-59

Shoe
Roger Vivier
circa 1959-61

Shoe
M & M Rayne Ltd.
circa 1968-70

Women's shoe styles are a sensitive barometer to the rise and fall of the hemline. Designed to complement the total look and balance a woman's proportions, they are continuously modified to meet the changes in fashion. The bulky, heavy styles of the war years, with their wedge heels, platform soles, and broad toes, echoed the masculine silhouette of women's clothing. However, the 1947 New Look demanded a more elegant look and shoe styles changed accordingly. Toes became more pointed, heels were slenderized and heightened, and the cut of the shoe changed to reveal more of the foot. By 1955, the stiletto shoe had arrived with its potentially destructive heel and pointed winkle-picker toe. As skirt lengths began to rise towards the end of the decade, women's shoes changed again. Heels were lowered, and rounded or squared toes gained in importance. The energy of youth in the 1960s brought with it an explosion of color and a taste for geometric lines. Chunky heels, broad toes, and platform soles appeared once again in updated versions.

Photograph 30

Hat
Yves Saint Laurent
circa 1962-67

Shoulder Bag
Roger Vivier
circa 1963-68

Boots
circa 1965-72

As hemlines continued to rise in the 1960s, all eyes were focused on legs — young legs. Patterned, textured, and wildly colored legs were on the move bringing with them the vogue for boots in all lengths and colors. In 1963 Vogue declared, "Boots, boots, and more boots are marching up and down like seven leagues, climbing to new leg lengths and taking with them stockings and kneesocks in thick depths of textures."

Color Plate 1

Blouse, Shorts, Two Skirts
Elizabeth Arden design by Castillo
circa 1946

Although Paris was widely acknowledged as the center of fashion throughout most of this century, a new breed of American-based designers gained importance during the 1940s and 1950s. The fact that the United States led the rest of the world in manufacturing and mass production techniques provided these designers with a tremendous advantage. Casual clothing, inspired by the Californian lifestyle, became known as the American image. Comfortable separates and coordinated sportswear, such as this four-piece outfit, were a welcome escape from the self-conscious haute couture. This design by Castillo consists of a blouse, undershorts, a short, pleated play skirt, and the dressier calf-length skirt pictured here.

Color Plate 2
Evening Gown and Cape
Elizabeth Arden design by Castillo
1946

The early 1940s' silhouette has sometimes been referred to as a square perched on top of a rectangle. This heavily padded cape and columnar skirt certainly reduced the human form to geometric proportions. The evening gown bodice and cape are heavily encrusted with an elaborate sequin trim. A separate panel forms a train at gown back.

Color Plate 3

Strapless Evening Gown
Bergdorf Goodman label
sold 1-12-51

At the end of World War II, women were urged to abandon
their involvement with the masculine world of work and get
back up on the pedestal. This movement, which culminated
in the mystique of femininity, encouraged a return to the
traditional sex-role stereotypes. Couturiers also looked backwards for design inspiration. This evening gown, with its draped
and pleated side panels, is reminiscent of the late 18th-century
fashion for drawing the overskirt up at the sides to reveal the
petticoat underneath.

Color Plate 4
Strapless Evening Gown
Christian Dior
1955

After Dior's New Look exploded on the fashion scene, women were told to "Get Yourself a New Shape." This meant emphasizing a shapely bosom, defining a small waist, and accentuating a rounded hipline. Couture designers eased the transition to this new silhouette by building shape into the inner construction of their creations. Based on individual measurements, they were made-to-order confections. This evening gown, with its sewn-in basque girdle, intricate underpadding, and five-layer stiffened petticoat, guaranteed a silhouette that was the essence of femininity.

Color Plate 5

Strapless Evening Gown
Balenciaga
circa 1950-55

This velvet and satin evening gown with three-layer petal skirt illustrates Balenciaga's sure sense of aesthetics and talent for creating stunning fashion images. His prices were high, sometimes the highest in Paris, but the results were moving sculptures. It was his knowledge of fabrics and his dressmaking skills which set Balenciaga apart from all other designers. Coco Chanel acknowledged this distinction when she said, "He is the only one who can cut, design, put-together and sew a suit or gown entirely alone."

Color Plate 6

Afternoon Dress
Christian Dior
1955

For the fashionable woman of the 1950s, accessories were an essential consideration. The decree that hats were as much a part of haute couture as the shape of the skirt or the cut of the bodice brought designers into the millinery arena. Balenciaga, Dior, Fath and others expanded the vocabulary of fashionable hats. As the trend accelerated, it became more time consuming and expensive to stay in vogue. Hats of the decade were either very small and perched on top of a neat chignon or very large, over-sized models. The half-Breton hat in this photograph is a Christian Dior design, circa 1952-56.

Color Plate 7

Two-piece Suit (left)
Jacques Fath
circa 1954

Three-piece Suit (right)
Christian Dior
1956

The severe, straight skirt and the graceful, full skirt on these two models illustrate the two signature silhouettes of the mid-1950s. Each shape had its proponents. The suit on the left is characteristic of its designer, Jacques Fath. He delighted in creating pencil-slim silhouettes; some were so restrictive that he had to add small slits in the skirt if women were to move at all. Fath's use of color was also distinctive. At a time when many designers favored deep, rich, dramatic shades, Fath preferred pretty pastel colors.

Color Plate 8
Evening Coat (left)
Christian Dior
1954

Evening Coat (right)
Christian Dior
1956

The voluminous cut of these tent-shaped evening coats provided a dramatic contrast to the figure-hugging silhouette of the Fifties' dress. The appearance of these coats is deceptively simple; they demanded expert shaping, seaming, and cutting. Note the differences in the hemline length. In 1956, Dior created a stir in the fashion world when he deviated from his practice in the previous years of gradually raising his hemlines. His Aimant, or Loving, collection in the fall of 1956 featured clothing which was romantic in feeling and featured a dropped hemline.

Color Plate 9
Strapless Gown
Christian Dior
1956

Purchasing a Dior original was a time-consuming task. Upon entering the salon, passports were examined to guard against design piracy. The favored viewers were then ushered into one of four salons for the showing. Approximately two hundred outfits (models) were shown taking about two hours. After selections were made, the customers were taken to the dressing rooms. Since only one model of each creation existed, a copy of the original was made expressly for the customer. If she couldn't fit into the model, a mannequin was brought in for a private showing. Generally, four fittings were required, based on over twenty measurements, to ensure, with painstaking exactness, that the dress was a perfect fit.

Color Plate 10
Strapless Dress (left)
Christian Dior
1960

Strapless Dress and Shawl (right)
Christian Dior
1965

The growing importance of the teenager during the 1950s encouraged a breakaway movement in fashion which celebrated youth. They wanted fashions that expressed their mood and uninhibited clothing to celebrate their liberation. The new cycle of fashions pushed skirt hemlines up to the knee by 1960 and up to the thigh by 1965. Revolutionary fashions were created by a new breed of youthful designers, such as Mary Quant. Established designers, who for years had catered to the mature woman, also began to listen to the voice of youth. These two evening dresses from the House of Dior combine the popularity of the shorter skirt with the couture tradition of luxurious fabrics and lavish trim.

Color Plate 11
Pants Suit
Emanuel Ungaro
circa 1967

Emanuel Ungaro trained under Cristobel Balenciaga from 1958 to 1963 and spent two seasons with André Courrèges before opening his own couture salon in 1965. Best known for his geometric designs, dramatic colors, and bold patterns, Ungaro once explained his mission as ''an attempt to nail down the contemporary spirit.'' In 1969, *Women's Wear Daily* described the Ungaro woman as Superwoman: tall, athletic, muscular, sunburned, and slightly terrifying. This pants suit, with its simple shapes, contrasting textures and vivid colors, represents Ungaro's architectural approach to the space-age fashions of the 1960s.

Color Plate 12

Leopard Skin Hat
DeLacy
circa 1944-47

Leopard Skin Purse
circa 1944-47

Shoes
Hanna Pope Co.
circa 1946-48

Color Plate 13

Umbrella
probably Elizabeth Arden, New York design by Castillo
circa 1947

Gloves
Elizabeth Arden, New York design by Castillo
1947

Hat
Elizabeth Arden, New York design by Castillo
circa 1947

During World War II, women's accessories became scarce and very costly. After the war, fashion embraced accessories with a passion. Tightly rolled umbrellas, hats, and gloves were all chosen with a discriminating eye. These accessories were probably designed by Castillo to complement his dress and jacket. See Photograph 9.

Catalogue of the Exhibition

Photographs:

1

Two Piece Suit (jacket and skirt)

Label: Adrian

circa 1942

Black wool "British Samek Material"; jacket with 3 button CF closure; turn down notched collar; button down shoulder yoke; 4 patch pockets; padded shoulders; silk lined. A-line skirt; unlined.

0.1048a,b

Hat

Label: DeLacy New York

circa 1944-47

Open crown wrapped turban; leopard skin lined with tan satin; inner reinforcing brown felt headband.

0.1158

Purse

circa 1944-47

Leopard skin and black calf leather lined with black suede; 2 expanding compartments and zippered case; matching leopard skin detachable bow.

0.1159a,b

2

Cocktail Dress

Label: Original Nat Tuman New York

circa 1940-42

Camel color, synthetic blend, tabby weave; dolman sleeve bodice with modified v-neckline; wrist closure with 5 covered buttons and fabric loops; beaded and sequinned U-shaped patch pocket at right hip; 2 gathered skirt panels attached to left front and back at waistline seam; padded shoulders; belt is not original to garment.

0.117

3

Two-Piece Suit (jacket and skirt)

Label: D. Veltry Fifth Avenue
New York

circa 1944

Mustard wool tailored jacket with black velvet trim; double-breasted with 8 velvet covered buttons and 4 bound buttonholes; turn down collar with peaked revers; 2 patch pockets; set-in sleeves with turn back cuffs trimmed in velvet; shoulder padding; diagonal seaming on back opens into 2 knife pleats; weighted hem; lined. Knee-length black wool skirt with contrast mustard wool trim; mod-

ified A-line; waist yoke panel with inset pocket; unlined.

0.1108,a,b

Hat

Label: Lorie registered model B
millinery Creators Guild

circa 1943

Black felt hat with shallow indented crown; 2 felt double looped bows decorate crown edge; 2 topstitched felt bands attached at hat edges to be worn across back of head; plain, full-faced black net veil.

0.1124

4

Day Dress, Jacket

Label: Milgrim

circa 1944

Short sleeve dress in tan and forest green printed silk; appliqued decorative cording on front shoulder yokes; shaped stand-up collar; wrap-around skirt pleated horizontally to create draping on right side. Forest green hip-length fitted jacket with flared hemline; topstitched shoulder yoke; sleeve and bodice constructed from one piece of fabric; padded shoulders; lined with dress fabric. Matching belt covered in dress fabric.

L82.20.195.34a,b,c

5

Close-up of Jacket

L82.20.195.34a,b,c

6

Close-up of Day Dress

L82.20.195.34a,b,c

7

Evening Gown

Label: Bergdorf Goodman X3309 Model
Moorin Sold 1/25/46

1946

Black nylon sleeveless gown with squared neckline and shirred bodice; boned midriff panel of black satin with appliqued and inset bands of pink silk in diamond pattern; straight sheath underskirt of black silk with side seam slits.

L82.20.213.52

Purse

Label: Morabito Paris

circa 1935-40

Black beaded evening bag; rhinestones decorate frame top; floral design in-

scribed on inside of gold metal frame; 4 interior pockets; black satin lining.

0.1201

8

Evening Coat

Label: Elizabeth Arden New York design
by Castillo

circa 1947

Cream silk faille fitted full-length coat; turn down notched collar with peaked revers; 4 button CF closure with bound buttonholes; flared skirt with 4 hipline vertical panels; padded shoulders; lined. Cream leather belt.

0.1103a,b

Clutch Purse (pochette)

circa 1940

Copper beaded purse; flap front closes with a snap; top-stitched outer edges; lined.

0.1201

9

Dress, Jacket (left)

Label: Elizabeth Arden New York design
by Castillo

1947

Blue silk dress with navy and white polka dots; discharge print; square neckline; full skirt gathered into waistline seam; short cap sleeves; set-in side seam pockets. Matching short jacket with navy velvet collar; set-in 3/4 length sleeves; 2 button CF closure with bound buttonholes; semi-attached deep folded overlay on back bodice; blue silk lining. Matching fabric covered belt. Fabric copyright 1947 on inner left side seam of dress. For matching gloves see color plate #13.

0.1106a,b,c,d,e

Hat

Label: Christian Dior Paris

circa 1947-55

Navy blue straw circular skimmer covered with navy brushed felt; brim edge and crown trimmed with navy grosgrain ribbon; flat double matching bow at crown CB.

0.1143

Coat (right)

Label: Elizabeth Arden New York

circa 1951

Navy wool fitted coat; turn down collar with revers; CF closure with 4 mother-of-pearl buttons and bound button-

holes; dropped zig-zag waistline seam; set-in pockets placed in hipline darts; flared skirt has 7 pressed inverted pleats; half lining.
0.1111

10
Two-Piece Suit (jacket and skirt)
Label: D. Veltry New York City
circa 1950-53
Black and white check silk taffeta fitted jacket with black velvet trim; turn down collar with revers; modified princess style seaming; CF closure with 3 velvet covered buttons and bound buttonholes; bound pockets; padded shoulders; black silk lining. Matching bias cut skirt, black silk lining. Black velvet belt with covered buckle.
0.1104a,b,c

Hat
Labels: Edgar Lorie Fifth Avenue New York
Florence Wilson Norfolk
circa 1947-54
Black felt modified half-Breton; trimmed with black satin ribbon and black feathers.
0.1135

11
Strapless Evening Gown
Label: Bergdorf Goodman New York
#61612 sold 1/12/51
1951
Off-white net decorated with floral pink and taupe beadwork; fitted curved bodice trimmed with net; built-in bodice stays; full skirt has 4 layers of netting; unfinished asymmetrical hemline; attached stiffened nylon petticoat.
0.1095

Gloves
circa 1947-57
Iridescent pink-lavender silk elbow-length gloves; elastic at inner wrist; unlined.
0.1200a,b

Necklace loaned by Linda Austin
Bracelet loaned by Mrs. L. Louise Cook

12
Strapless Evening Gown
Label: Bergdorf Goodman New York
#61611 sold 1/12/51
1951
Silver-gray silk satin gown with fitted turn down bodice; curved V-line at CB;

bias cut skirt has trapunto decoration stitched with silver metallic thread; attached bra cups; lined bodice.
L82.20.181.20

Gloves
Label: Frivolités de Jacques Fath
circa 1950-55
Powder blue silk satin above-the-elbow evening gloves, elastic at inner wrist; unlined.
0.1199a,b

Necklace and pin loaned by Mrs. L. Louise Cook
Earrings loaned by Mrs. Aileen B. Beresford.

13
Strapless Evening Gown
Label: Bergdorf Goodman New York
#61616 sold 1/12/51
1951
Amethyst silk faille and slate gray peau de soie; curved bodice with pleated panels that cross diagonally; attached pleated cummerbund; floor-length wrapped skirt with curved hemline; 4 separate panels of varying lengths drape over skirt at back and sides; metal built-in bodice stays; attached bra cups.
0.1096

14
Strapless Evening Gown, Shoulder Wrap
Label: Bergdorf Goodman New York
#61617 sold 1/12/51
1951
Black silk taffeta with satin stripes; curved bodice with CF tucks; floor-length circular bias cut skirt with asymmetrical hemline; built-in bodice stays; attached bra cups; lined bodice. Rectangle of matching fabric folded and stitched to create wrap-around shoulder covering with 3/4-length sleeves; unlined. Matching fabric tie belt.
L82.20.229.68a,b,c

Necklace loaned by Mrs. L. Louise Cook

15
Bodice and Skirt
Label: Christian Dior Paris #44075
Spring/Summer 1954
1954
Black silk figured weave; sleeveless bodice with shoulder pleats; V-neckline with

revers; 4 button CB closure with bound buttonholes; lined. Matching A-line skirt; 2 inverted pleats in skirt front; weighted hem; lined.
L82.20.233.72a,b

Hat
Label: Jean Desses 17 Avenue Matignon
Paris "Made in France"
circa 1950-55
Large cartwheel hat of pleated black organdy over straw form; low rounded crown; wide circular brim; plastic comb attached at CF inner band.
0.1136a

Jewelry loaned by Mrs. L. Louise Cook

16
Bodice and Skirt
Label: Christian Dior Paris #44076
Spring/Summer 1954
1954
Short sleeve cream linen bodice with notched shawl collar; set-in sleeves; 3 button CF closure with bound buttonholes; 2 silk peplums attached at waistline, 1 with stays; hand sewn seam finishes; muslin lining. Matching straight skirt; muslin lining. Matching shaped tie belt; hook and eye fastenings. Ecru silk half slip.
L.82.20.241.80a,b,c,d

Hat
Labels: Mr. John
Montaldo's
circa 1960
Small pillbox hat of sea green and cream organdy quilted in green thread; matching flat bow attached to left side.
0.1152

Jewelry loaned by Mrs. L. Louise Cook

17
Cocktail Dress
circa 1950-55
Charcoal silk dress with wrapped bodice pleated at right side seam; dropped waistline comes to a point at CF; 3/4-length set-in sleeves; full circular skirt gathered into waistline seam; unlined. Black silk faille full-length slip; A-line style; attached bra cups.
L82.20.248.87a,b

Jewelry loaned by Mrs. L. Louise Cook

18

Afternoon Dress

circa 1955

Beige silk faille fitted dress; elbow-length dolman sleeves with peaked cuffs; double shawl collar separates at CB; surplice bodice with left front 3 button closure; skirt fabric shirred at zipper on left front hip to create draping and modified bustle at CB; inner tape extends from waist to hipline to maintain shape; left front slit; unlined.
0.1114

Hat

Labels: Milgrim
          Florence Wilson Norfolk
circa 1950-55

Small Juliet cap with curved front edge; brown velour decorated with beadwork; 1/2 face brown veil; plastic comb at inner CF edge.
0.1131

Jewelry loaned by Linda Austin

19

Cocktail Dress

Label: Hattie Carnegie
circa 1953-56

Black silk jacquard weave; curved and pleated bodice with corded shoulder straps; skirt is gathered and pleated at back hipline; attached bra cups; unlined. Matching shaped tie belt.
0.1097a,b

Jewelry loaned by Mrs. L. Louise Cook

20

Evening Coat

Label: Balenciaga 10 Avenue George V
          Paris
circa 1950-55

Pale green velvet circular clutch coat; turn down cape collar extends to waist at CB; curved hemline; 3/4-length sleeves; lined.
0.1110

Hat

Labels: Mr. John
          Montaldo's
circa 1953-56

Deep sea green plush velvet turban on mesh form; 2 plastic combs at inner edge; kelly green silk lining.
0.1142

21

Coat

Label: Christian Dior Paris #75919
          Fall/Winter 1955
1955

Red wool with raised nap; double breasted with 8 button closure and machine-worked buttonholes; set-in sleeves with wrist placket closure; stand-away band collar; princess style back with 2 set-in skirt pleats; lined.
L82.20.231.70

22

Strapless Gown

Label: Christian Dior Paris #83090
          Fall/Winter 1956
1956

Pale green velvet with wrapped metallic silver and green embroidery; fitted bodice; flared skirt; attached strapless slip with boned bodice and crinoline petticoat.
0.1062

Fan

circa 1900-1910

Full, half-circle ostrich feather fan on ivory sticks; attached ivory-colored tassel.
0.1198

Jewelry loaned by Cynthia McCoy

23

Strapless Gown

Label: Christian Dior Paris #102723
          Fall/Winter 1959
1959

White net decorated with clear drop beads, silver sequins, round and leaf-shaped silver paillettes and rhinestones; fitted straight-edged bodice; full waltz-length skirt with asymmetrical hemline; skirt has 5 layers of alternating plain and decorated net; semi-attached waistline belt, attached petticoat; built-in metal bodice stays.
0.1093

Jewelry loaned by Mrs. Aideen B. Beresford

24

**Three-Piece Suit
(jacket, skirt, blouse)**

Label: Balenciage 10 Avenue George V
          Paris
1963

Black silk blouson jacket with diagonal armseye opening; back shoulder extension forms front yoke; 7 button CF closure with bound buttonholes; curved hemline dips at CB; semi-attached lining of jacket back is weighted. Matching A-line skirt; lined. White linen sleeveless blouse; scoop neckline; pleated shoulder seams; asymmetrical left front closure with 4 buttons and bound buttonholes; curved hemline dips at CB.
0.113a,b,c

25

Evening Gown

Label: Courreges Paris
circa 1963

Beige silk with pale peach organdy overlay and white vinyl trim; sleeveless bodice has square neckline and scooped armseye; broad vinyl midriff band; matching vinyl band at hemline; all over pattern of diamond shaped vinyl appliques with circular extensions.
0.1100

26

Dress

Label: Yves Saint Laurent Paris #013767
1966

Shocking pink wool knit bodice; sleeveless; top-stitched collar band and front bodice yoke; vertical side panels; dropped waistline; attached black kid leather skirt; above-the-knee hemline; A-line silhouette; silk lined. Matching black leather belt with silver buckle.
0.1098a,b

Hat

Label: An Original by Dajon New York
circa 1966

Black and white grosgrain beret; 36 sections radiate from crown center that is decorated with a wide fabric loop; narrow brim; tan silk lined.
0.1156

27

Dress

Label: Yves Saint Laurent Paris #015494
circa 1965

Multi-colored abstract African raw silk print; A-line shift; rectangular armseye formed by side panels; round neckline trimmed with turn down collar; collar decoration includes a wide variety of colored wooden, glass and plastic beads with embroidery stitches; yellow silk free-hanging lining.
0.1101

28

Hat (top left)
Label: Balenciaga 10 Avenue George V.
        Paris
circa 1956-60

Pale sea green swiss-braid straw with matching sea green silk scarf; souwester style; high, rounded crown lined with 2 layers of white net.
0.1150

Hat (center left)
Label: Schiaparelli Paris
circa 1953-56

Small circular black satin pill-box hat; satin gathered into folds at crown center; 1/2 face veil with decorative scallop stitching; black sequins attached to left and right crown and sides in a floral design; black silk taffeta lining.
0.1145

Hat (bottom left)
Labels: Milgrim
         Florence Wilson Norfolk
circa 1950-55

Deep sea green plush velvet turban on mesh form; 2 plastic combs at inner edge; kelly green silk lining.
0.1131

Hat (top right)
Label: Florence Wilson Norfolk
circa 1949-54

Black straw beret; black grosgrain curved trim stitched on hat edge in front and sides; 1/2 face decorative veil; matching straw "feather" attached at right front edge backed with grosgrain and quill; plastic comb at front rim.
0.1134

Hat (center right)
Label: Florence Wilson Norfolk
circa 1947-53

Low crowned black felt hat; brim and crown made from one piece; brim extends 2 1/2" in front, 1/2" at back; back shaped headband; velvet bow at back crown.
0.1132

Hat (bottom right)
Label: Strictly from Unger New York
circa 1955-59

Black crinoline flower pot hat covered with black downy feathers; turquoise velvet bow attached at front.
0.1144

29 (from left to right)

Shoes
Label: Florsheim
circa 1940-45

Black suede court shoe; decorative top-stitched crossover at toe; almond toe with cut-out peep toe opening; 2 7/8" heel; decorative suede buckle.
0.1168a,b

Shoes
Label: Massaro Opera 70-23 12 Rue de
        la Paix Paris
circa 1949-54

Maroon satin covered court shoe with almond toe; extra fabric gathered across toe into rhinestone clasp; 2 3/4" continental heel.
0.1189a,b

Shoes
Label: Designer Originals Jacqueline
circa 1950-55

Black synthetic pump, almond toe; decorative bow attached at toe, tapered 3 1/4" heel; back of shoe lined with split pink leather.
Loaned by Iva Sebra

Shoes
Label: Hofheimer's Cavalier deLuxe
circa 1955-59

Black patent leather court shoe, 3 1/2" stiletto heel; low-cut winkle picker toes.
0.1172a,b

Shoes
Label: Roger Vivier Paris
circa 1959-61

Black peau de soie covered with black lace and black sequins in a striped pattern; narrow rouleau black tie bow at toe; 2 5/8" comma heel; winkle picker toe.
0.1170a,b

Shoes
Label: M & M Rayne Ltd.
        "By appointment of H.M. The
        Queen Shoemakers"
circa 1968-70

Bright orange fabric with clear plastic trim; geometric styling; 3" chunky heel; 1/4" platform toe.
0.1187a,b

30

Hat
Label: Yves Saint Laurent Paris New York
        "Madrigal Imported Body Made
        in Italy" stamped on crown
circa 1962-67

Copper-colored brushed felt hat with deep crown and floppy brim; crown and brim constructed of one piece; black braid trim also forms the YSL trademark monogram on crown CF.
0.1157

Shoulder Bag
Label: Roger Vivier Paris
circa 1963-68

Cream patent leather bag with shoulder strap attached to frame by large white plastic loops; kid leather change purse with flap attached to interior pocket; white moire lining.
0.1196

Boot
Label: Yves Saint Laurent Paris
circa 1968-72

Navy blue suede lined with rust-colored leather; below-the-knee boot with squared, almond toe; 2 7/8" heel; inner leg zipper on boot stocking.
0.1192a,b

Boot
No Label
circa 1966-71

Lilac weft single-knit fabric; black elasticized lining; squared, almond toe; 2 3/8" heel.
0.1193a,b

Boot
No Label
circa 1968-72

Stocking boot of white stretch knit fabric; squared toe; Made in Italy stamped on leather sole; chunky, fabric-covered 2 7/8" heel; unlined.
0.1195a,b

Boot
No Label
circa 1964-70

Black, "Wet-Look" vinyl; squared toe; inner leg zipper extends to boot top; square rubber 1 5/8" heel, ecru double knit lining.
0.1194a,b

Color Plates:

1

Blouse, Shorts, Two Skirts
Label: Elizabeth Arden New York design
by Castillo
circa 1946

Red and white stripe silk short sleeve blouse; turn down collar with revers; set-in sleeves with turn back cuffs; 6 button CF closure with bound buttonholes; matching undershorts; high cut leg opening with self fabric bias piping; crotch gusset. Matching above-the-knee play skirt; knife pleats; set-in side seam pockets; fabric selvage forms lower edge. Matching calf-length skirt with shaped high-rise waistband; wrap-around style.
0.1109a,b,c,d

2

Evening Gown, Cape
Label: Elizabeth Arden New York design
by Castillo
1946

Black silk crepe gown; sleeveless bodice with pleated shoulder straps; powder blue sequinned applied design decorates bodice front; floor-length skirt with deep CB vent; skirt over-panel attached at back waistline and side seams; attached bra cups; partial bodice lining. Powder blue silk faille short cape with matching sequin decoration; collarless; padded shoulders; lined.
0.1115a,b,c

Gloves
Label: Frivolitiés de Jacques Fath
circa 1950-55

Powder blue silk satin above-the-elbow evening gloves, elastic at inner wrist; unlined.
0.1199a,b

3

Strapless Evening Gown
Label: Bergdorf Goodman New York
#61614 sold 1/12/51
1951

Turquoise silk satin; fitted bodice with pleated band around upper edge; full skirt has pleated draping across hipline and gathered polonnaise overskirt; pleated train falls from back waistline seam; built-in bodice stays; attached bra cups; attached silk half-slip. Matching

covered belt; stamped in gold on inner side of belt "Nettie Rosenstein 14."
0.1094a,b

Earrings, necklace, and bracelet loaned by Mrs. Aideen B. Beresford.
Pin and gloves loaned by Mrs. L. Louise Cook.

4

Strapless Evening Gown
Label: Christian Dior Paris #75917
Fall/Winter 1955
1955

Pale peach silk satin with silver embroidered and sequinned overlay of pale gray-silver net. Fitted bodice with metallic trim border; bell-shaped skirt has attached 5 layer crinoline and buckram petticoat; interlining of silver georgette; built-in bodice corset with metal stays.
0.1092

Jewelry loaned by Mrs. Aideen B. Beresford

5

Strapless Evening Gown
Label: Balenciaga 10 Avenue George V
Paris
circa 1950-55

Purple silk satin and velvet; bodice has asymmetrical left front button closure and curved turn down edge; 3 layer skirt comprised of a straight satin skirt, satin underskirt of curved panels, and 2 curved velvet overskirt panels; asymmetrical hemline, built-in bodice stays.
0.1105

Earrings and pin loaned by Mrs. Aileen B. Beresford
Gloves loaned by Mrs. L. Louise Cook
Necklace loaned by Cynthia McCoy

6

Afternoon Dress
Label: Christian Dior Paris #53572
Spring/Summer 1955
1955

Printed silk with yellow, gray, and aubergine floral design; waltz-length; pleated cowl neckline drops to a V at CF; 3/4-length set-in sleeves; full gathered skirt; attached underslip with 2 layer dropped waist organdy petticoat. Matching covered belt; additional brown suede belt.
L82.20.232.71a,b,c

Hat
Label: Christian Dior Paris
circa 1952-56

Half-Breton straw hat; rounded crown and wide brim; yellow silk rib faille trim at crown base; glass, beads, and rhinestones in silver setting comprise pin at CB; plastic comb at CF inner rim.
0.1149

Jewelry loaned by Linda Austin

7

Two-Piece Suit
(jacket and skirt) (left)
Label: Jacques Fath Paris
circa 1954

Pink raw silk fitted jacket; 3/4-length set-in sleeves; turn down collar with revers decorated with lapel flaps and pink plastic buttons; 5 button CF closure with bound buttonholes; lined. Matching straight skirt; 8 waistline darts, lined.
L82.20.245.84a,b

Hat
Label: Florence Wilson Norfolk
circa 1950

Black felt hat; low crown; back of hat has shaped felt headband; large velvet bow at top of crown.
0.1132

Jewelry loaned by Mrs. L. Louise Cook

Three-Piece Suit
(jacket, skirt, and bodice) (right)
Label: Christian Dior Paris #'s 81128 &
81129 Spring/Summer 1956
1956

Pink and rose floral silk print; sleeveless bodice; square neckline; lining with stays extends below bodice hemline to form a peplum. Matching short sleeve bolero jacket; turn down collar; jacket back, shoulders, and sleeve back cut in 1 piece; weighted hem; ecru silk lined. Matching skirt with box pleats; organdy lined. Matching covered shaped belt.
L82.20.238.77a,b,c,d

Jewelry loaned by Linda Austin

8

Evening Coat (left)
Label: Christian Dior Paris #40619
Spring/Summer 1954
1954

Black silk faille taffeta tent coat; cape shawl collar squared at back; 3/4-length

full set-in sleeves with 2 pleats at arms-eye seam; coat back gathered with 6 box pleats, lined.
L82.20.207.46

Jewelry loaned by Mrs. Aileen B. Beresford

Evening Coat (right)
Label: Christian Dior Paris #84070
Fall/Winter 1956
1956

Bright green silk taffeta tent clutch coat; 3/4-length, modified bell, set-in sleeves; stand-up collar; 2 large front patch pockets with flaps; waltz-length.
L82.20.206.45

Hat
Label: Jean Desses 17 Avenue Matignon Paris "Made in France"
circa 1950-55

Large cartwheel hat of pleated black organdy over straw form; low rounded crown; wide circular brim, plastic comb attached at CF inner band.
0.1136a

9
Strapless Gown
Label: Christian Dior Paris #83093
Fall/Winter 1956
1956

Gold and silver lame in graduated geometric design; waltz-length gown; inset skirt front panel; attached strapless slip with boned bodice and crinoline petticoat. Gold lame pleated cummerbund.
0.1072a,b

Jewelry loaned by Mrs. Aileen B. Beresford.

10
Strapless Dress (left)
Label: Christian Dior Paris #104987
Spring/Summer 1960
1960

Off-white net decorated with white embroidered cotton open work overlay in floral design; embroidered work arranged in overlapping patterns to create 3-dimensional effect; curved bodice; semi-fitted waist with flared skirt; built-in corset with attached garters; crinoline petticoat; attached silk underslip.
0.1091

Jewelry loaned by Mrs. Aileen B. Beresford.

Strapless Dress and Shawl (right)
Label: Christian Dior Paris #127105
Spring/Summer 1965
1965

Bright purple silk crepe with gold and purple jewelled passementerie trim; sheath style; wrap-around back panel with attached bow; lower edge of dress and back panel decorated with passementerie trim; built-in corset with attached garters, purple silk lined. Semi-circular matching capelet; lower edge decorated with passementerie trim.
0.1063a,b

11
Pants Suit (tunic and pants)
Label: Emanuel Ungaro Couture Paris
circa 1967-69
Gift of Mrs. Gwynne Garbisch McDevitt
Black cotton decorated with all-over abstract multi-colored floral pattern of vinyl appliques and decorative stitching; sleeveless, hip-length tunic; shaped collarless neckline; black silk lined. Matching bell-bottomed pants, hip-hugger style; no waistband; CF zipper closure; black silk lined.
0.1102a,b

12
Hat
Label: DeLacy
circa 1944-47

Open crown wrapped turban; leopard skin lined with tan satin; inner reinforcing brown felt headband.
0.1158

Purse
No Label
circa 1944-47

Leopard skin and black calf leather lined with black suede; 2 expanding compartments and zippered case; matching leopard skin detachable bow.
0.1159a,b
0.1159a,b

Shoes
Label: Hanna Pope Co. Paramount Style Shoes
circa 1946-48

Tan leather pumps with squareish toe; plastic covered wooden heel, 3 1/8" Boulevard heel; decorative stitching on toe.
0.1183a,b

13
Umbrella
Label: No Label, probably Elizabeth Arden New York design by Castillo
circa 1947

Navy blue and white striped silk seamed at each spoke to form V-patterns; selvage forms outer edge; metal spokes; cherry stained wooden handle decorated with matching ruched fabric; umbrella held closed with button, metal circular loop, and fabric band.
0.1185

Gloves
Label: No Label, Elizabeth Arden New York design by Castillo
1947

Blue and white polka dot silk gloves; whip-stitched outer edges; gloves match dress and jacket. 0.1106a,b; see Photograph 12.
0.1106e,d

Hat
Label: Elizabeth Arden New York design by Castillo
circa 1947

Navy blue and white striped silk open crown elliptical hat; tied matching bow at CB; white silk lined.
0.1139

Not Illustrated:
Hostess Gown
Label: Elizabeth Arden New York design by Castillo
1946

Iridescent gray silk taffeta gown with surplice front and funnel neckline; pleated bell sleeves; diamond-shaped back bodice; triangular hipline yoke; attached pleated cummerbund encircles hips; padded shoulders, partial bodice lining.
L82.20.228.67

Afternoon Dress, Jacket
Label: Elizabeth Arden New York design by Castillo
1946

Chocolate linen strapless waltz-length dress; interlaced curved bands of fabric form figure-8 design along bodice; flared skirt decorated with large appliqued ecru linen coin dots; scalloped ecru hemline border; built-in bodice stays. Matching short jacket with turn down collar and buttoned surplice front closure; raglan short sleeves; padded shoulders.
0.1112a,b

Strapless Dress
Label: Christian Dior Paris #53577
      Spring/Summer 1955
1955
Waltz-length dress; ecru silk with violet and taupe floral warp print; organdy lined pleated full skirt; attached crinoline petticoat; built-in bodice stays; lined. Matching pleated sash attached at left front and draped diagonally across bodice.
0.1054a,b

Evening Coat
Label: Christian Dior Paris #53578
      Spring/Summer 1955
1955
Tent silhouette, waltz-length coat; ecru silk organza with violet and taupe floral warp print; semi-attached shawl collar; unpressed pleats on coat front; 3/4-length set-in sleeves; lining and interlining of net; to be worn with 0.1054a,b.
0.1055

Dress
Label: Yves Saint Laurent Paris #10494
1965
Mondrian-inspired, red, yellow and black geometric design on a cream silk background; modified scoop neckline; rectangular armseye; above-the-knee hemline; fully lined.
0.1099

Coat
Label: Yves Saint Laurent Paris #013767
1966
Black kid leather A-line coat; double-breasted with 8 buttons and bound buttonholes; notched turn down collar; 2 patch pockets; dropped waistline; princess style seaming; set-in sleeves with wrist placket closure; sleeve edges, collar and pocket flaps trimmed with black mink; lined.
0.1098c

All costumes, unless otherwise noted, are from the collection of Jean Outland Chrysler.